Radio Daze

A DESCENT INTO COLLECTING

Radio Daze
A DESCENT INTO COLLECTING

Aaron Zevy

ISBN: 9781739023706

Printed in Canada

COPYRIGHT

Edited by Jules Lewis
Copy edit by Miles Dorfman
Cover design by Tatiana Sayig
Book layout by Helen Prancic
Photography by Aaron Zevy, Decophobia

The cover image of this book, as well as the images shown within the story '1956 Hallicrafters in Dijon Yellow' were modified using tools found on Picsart.com.

CONTENTS

INTRODUCTION

After writing three short story collections in a little over a year, I stopped writing.

Soon after, I started collecting radios.

Replacing one obsession, one might say, with another.

I do not know why.

I had never seen any of these radios before.

They did not remind me of gentler or simpler times.

They were, I thought, I think, just beautiful.

The colors and the designs.

If it was more than that, well, I suppose that would be a question for my revolving team of shrinks and therapists.

These radios brought me a great amount of joy and pleasure.

As I had recently fallen under the malady of the dreaded 'writer's block', a lot of friends and family thought themselves very clever by suggesting I should start writing about collecting radios.

As if it were that easy.

These, by the way, were the same people who suggested I use my Peloton for something other than hanging wet towels.

Someone even had the temerity to use the line "if these radios could talk, oh what stories they could tell."

I threw that person out of my house. Let the radios be, I pleaded.

Let them sit on their shelves, and let them sing their songs of unbearable static.

They were not literary devices.

They were not writing exercises.

They were just old radios.

And then, as you may have guessed, I wrote a story. And then another.

And then this book.

I'm not saying that's a good thing. Enjoy.

THE RADIO CONTEST

The Zevys ate dinner at 6:00. Not at 6:05.
Not at 6:09.
Not, heaven forbid, at 6:15. We ate dinner at 6:00.

If you asked my bubby at 5:59 if she were hungry, she would look at the clock and shake her head no in a way which intimated that it was the craziest question she had ever heard.

But at 6:00, she was famished.

Aside from the precise starting time, my father had two important rules about dinner which we had to abide:

1. You had to finish everything on your plate.

2. You could not answer the phone.

Now, if you are envisioning a long elaborate dinner ending with dessert and a cheese plate, then you may have stumbled into the wrong house.

Dinner was over by 6:30.

Unless, of course, you were having a problem with rule number 1.

Then it was over whenever you finished your plate.

I once sat with twenty-two green peas, I had plenty of time to count them, until 8:15.

I eventually finished them, with the help of my mother, who, may she rest in peace, may have had a forkful or two.

But this story is not about food. It is about rule number 2.

Both my siblings and I have romanticized thoughts and memories of our parents. I think that is a good thing. The three of us don't have to embellish or exaggerate the past because we were blessed to have had amazing parents.

Now, my brother Dov is five years younger than me. One of the things he loves to tell people about my father is that he would answer the phone with the traditional Italian salutation of 'pronto'.

Which is true.

He was not Italian. It was just his schtick.

The thing is, because Dov is five years younger, in 1973 he would have been 9 years old and nobody he knew was calling him on the phone. Least of all, between 6:00 and 6:30.

Because if they had, they would have heard what my friends, the biggest culprit being Stevie Sheen who reveled in my entire ordeal, heard when my father, quite a bit irritated, answered the phone.

He did not say pronto. He did not say hello.

What he would say, in either French or English depending on his mood or disposition, was:

"What time do you have dinner at your house?"

And then, after what was surely a moment of stunned silence, "Ronnie can't come to the phone."

Then he would calmly hang up and go back to his plate of spaghetti.

So that's what I remember.

Which was all well and good and I guess at the time more than a little embarrassing, but it would not have been a big deal if Jethro Tull had not come to town.

Those of you of a certain age will know that Jethro Tull is a 1970s rock band. You will also know that there were no Jethros or any Tulls and that the lead singer's name was Ian Anderson.

One of the gifts I had received for my bar mitzvah was a Sanyo cassette deck, and my cousin David recorded two albums for me on my very first cassette. On one side was Santana's Abraxas And on the other, was Aqualung by Jethro Tull.

It is now nearly 50 years later and I still get a kick out of the lyrics 'snot is running down his nose.'

I wanted to go to the concert.

Badly.

But I did not have tickets.

My only hope was a contest being run by the local Montreal AM radio station CKGM.

CKGM was the AM top 40 station in the city, and their two big name disc jockeys were Ralph the Birdman Lockwood and Marc 'mais oui' Denis.

In 1973 they ran contests the entire year. Sometimes for cash prizes up to $1000, and sometimes for concert tickets.

The concept was easy.

You would send in postcards to the radio station with your phone number. Then, the whole week before the concert, every hour between 4 and 8, the DJ would pick a postcard and dial the number.

All you had to do was answer the phone and say "I listen to CKGM."

Like I said. Easy.

I had inundated the radio station with postcards. So had Stevie Sheen. We had planned to go together if either of us won. Now, in order to enlist my sister's help, I might have promised her a ticket too. But I would cross that proverbial bridge when I had to.

Since my bubby never answered the phone, I now had my brother, sister, and even mother, who had a little trouble remembering the call letters and tried, unsuccessfully, to convince us it would be ok to just say "I listen to the radio," instead, now covering the 4-8 time slot.

The only problem was dinner. 6:00 to 6:30.

My father, though strict and serious, was a kind, generous, and very fair man. He was honest to a fault and had a dry sense of humor which my friends, after overcoming their initial fear and trepidation, came to appreciate and enjoy.

But he was never, ever, ever going to answer the phone by saying, "I listen to CKGM."

Not that we didn't ask.

Not that we didn't plead.

Not that we didn't beg.

But it was never going to happen.

He wouldn't even engage us in conversation. He found the whole thing ludicrous and not even worthy of his attention.

My mom even tried and his answer, in English, was the only time he ever addressed it directly. He said, "But I don't listen to CKGM."

Which, for him, ended matters.

As luck would have it, the phone did not ring once between 6:00 and 6:30 that week.

And, as luck would also have it, the radio station never called at any other time either.

My mother, after tiring of explaining it to her friends and relatives, quit after the third day. I think I may have even heard my sister say hello once or twice.

I never saw Jethro Tull.

For a couple of weeks after the concert, whenever the phone rang during dinner, we would wait and see if my father would make a joke.

But he never did.

After a while, although there were still contests, we just forgot about it.

About a month later, we convinced my mother to take us to McDonald's for dinner. It was a huge treat.

My father, surprisingly, did not hate McDonald's. In fact, if memory serves, he was a big fan of their French Fries. But that night my bubby, his mother, was feeling a little tired so it was just the three kids and my mom.

When we got back, French Fries in tow for my father, he waved a notepad at me.

"Aaron," he said, "you got a phone call while you were gone."

It was not like my father to write down messages from Stevie Sheen.

"From who?" I asked.

My father looked down at the pad and said, "from a Mr. Ralph Lockwood from CKGM," he said.

My sister squealed, "Oh my god!!! Oh my god!!"

I was but a year older than my sister, but, in my mind, many years wiser.

"What was the message?"

My father looked down again. Then he looked up.

"Usually at around 8:30," he said.

My sister said "What????"

I turned to her and said.

"Danielle, that is when Ralph Lockwood has dinner at his house."

My father nodded, smiled, and took the French Fries from my hand.

1938 EMERSON BULLSEYE

Allie has told me not to mention my radios until the third or fourth date.

"Fourth," she says, correcting herself, "not until the fourth."

"What if she comes over?" I ask. "How am I supposed to explain all the radios on the shelves? Am I holding them for a friend?"

"Don't flatter yourself," she retorts, "nobody is coming over."

"Can I tell the story about the Sparton Sled? About how I returned it."

"No."

"But it makes me look down to earth."

"It doesn't. It makes you look like a kook."

"Love the support," I say. "So, what do I talk about?"

"Her," she says, "ask her questions about herself."

I'm going out on my first blind date in a long time. Allie has called to give me a pep talk. So far, it hasn't been too peppy.

"No radios?" I ask.

"No," she replies, "if I trusted you to mention it casually, just in passing, I would say ok. But you can't help yourself. You are going to launch into a thirty-minute speech about the history of catalin."

"That speech is very informative," I counter.

"I'm thinking of giving a Ted Talk."

"No radios. Don't even turn on the radio in the car."

Linda Horvath was a lawyer in Miami. She was divorced with kids long out of the house. We had exchanged very pleasant texts and now we were meeting for drinks at a hip restaurant in the Design District.

My plan, as per Allie, was to ask a lot of questions and to show a lot of interest. How hard could that be?

"Are you working on an interesting file?" I asked when our mojitos arrived.

"Very," she replied after taking her first sip. "I'm representing the heirs of a Jewish family from France who had their art looted by the Nazis."

"Wow, that is really interesting," I said, repeating the line I had practiced in front of the mirror in case what she told me was not interesting at all. But this was actually interesting.

"It is. But it is painstaking work."

"How do you mean?"

"Right now, I am going through online photo albums of pictures taken of Parisian apartments. Trying to match up the art on the wall with art we suspect was looted."

"You do that?" I asked incredulously.

"Yes."

"Why not a law clerk?" I asked.

"Because they don't have a Masters in Art History," she said with a smile.

"Well played counselor," I said.

This asking question stuff was a breeze. I could go weeks without mentioning radios.

I decided to step on the gas.

"I'm not sure if they are privileged," I said using a word I had heard on a TV law show, "but I would love to see some of those photos. I don't have a Masters in Art history but I once had to use the bathroom at the MoMA."

She laughed and said, "if you are really interested, I have some on my phone. But not if you are faking."

"I'm really interested," I replied, "the faking is for later." Another laugh.

She grabbed her phone and scrolled through some pictures. Then slid her chair a little closer to mine.

"This is a picture taken in the Grundfelt apartment in the 13th arrondissement of Paris in 1940. Just before the Nazi stormed in. And this," she pinched at the screen of the iPhone in order to stretch a picture, "is a Klimt on the living room wall. We believe it is the same painting now owned by a well-known Silicon Valley CEO."

"Do you know the provenance?" I was just killing it with my art world knowledge.

"Not entirely clear," she replied, "but it was sold at auction by a German art dealer. Along with some other pieces we suspect were looted."

"Wow!" I said again. "This could be a movie."

Then we spent about ten flirty minutes talking about who would play her in the movie. I, of course, was suggesting extremely attractive actresses.

"Do you want to see another before I put the phone away?" she asked.

"Sure," I said.

She swiped once and handed me the phone "this one is a Renoir," she said.

"Hey, not fair," I retorted with a fake pout, "I would have gotten that one."

"I'm sure you would have," she said with a laugh. Has anyone been counting the laughs?

"I'm sure you will get some more chances to display all the knowledge you gained in the MoMA bathroom."

I took the phone and looked at the picture.

I definitely would have recognized the Renoir. I think.

But I wasn't looking at the painting. Because, below the painting was a desk. A beautiful art deco desk. And on the desk was a radio. Now I pinched the screen as she had to zoom in on it. The picture was grainy but the design was the unmistakable and stunning Sakhnoffsky design of the 1938 Emerson Bullseye.

I knew because I had one on my shelf.

"That's an Emerson," I said out loud, mostly to myself.

"Pretty sure it's a Renoir," she replied - not laughing as hard this time.

"1938 Emerson designed by Count Alexis de Sakhnoffsky," I said showing off confidently. "American made, but Emersons, and this model in particular, were very popular amongst the upper classes in Europe at the time."

"What are you talking about?"

I showed her the zoomed-in image of the Emerson "The radio on the desk. It is a 1938 Emerson."

"How do you know so much about radios?"

Allie in a devil's suit was sitting on my shoulder wagging her finger. "I don't know that much," I said. "I think I may have seen it in a book."

"A book about radios?" she asked incredulously.

"It might have been something about Art Deco," I replied.

"That makes sense," she said nodding her head, "because an entire book devoted to radios sounds a little bit crazy."

I laughed and looked at the picture again. There was something very familiar about this radio. I zoomed to a spot on the top right corner. The wood had been chipped and left a very distinctive mark. There were three jagged edges. They looked like the peaks of three mountains.

My heart skipped a beat. I was pretty sure I knew this radio.

When we said our goodbyes, me with a perfunctory kiss on the cheek, I asked Linda if she could email me the picture. She said of course.

In an hour, I would be home and compare the crack in the picture with the one that my Emerson had.

In an hour and ten minutes, I would conclude that the 1938 Emerson Bullseye with the Ingraham cabinet displayed on a shelf in my Boca Raton home, had very likely been looted in 1940 along with the Renoir from an apartment in Paris.

I had seen the radio in books and on Pinterest. I didn't really collect wood radios but the deep wood grain and the layers of circle in the chassis were mesmerizing. It had been designed by Count Alexis de Sakhnoffsky. I didn't know who he was either but it sure sounded cool.

I wanted one but had only ever seen one for sale. There was one available on eBay. I had scrolled to the listing many times. It had been there for months and nobody had bought it. Not a good sign. In part, I think, because the price was really inflated. In part because the seller was in Europe and the shipping and insurance costs were high and, in part because of the chip. Collectors, and I vainly thought of myself as one, cared about the appearance of the set. This radio had a pretty prominent chip. So, I never really considered it seriously. The listing said that it 'worked' but that could mean anything. And then, maybe realizing his ad was clearly not getting any traction, one day he added a video to the description. You could click on it and be redirected to YouTube. The Emerson, crack and all, played beautifully. The clip was about thirty seconds of a Beethoven piano concerto. Almost no static at all. I recognized the piece. It was one of my father's favorites. After the video went up, I checked every couple of days and the radio was still there. None of my other dealers had one for sale. So, fearful that I would never see another working copy and, convincing myself that the crack didn't really bother me, I bought it. When it arrived, I displayed it proudly and prominently on a shelf in the living room. From the couch, you couldn't notice either the chip or its murky provenance. I really loved that radio.

I called Allie.

"How bad was it?" she asked.

"Not bad at all," I replied.

"What did you talk about?" she asked.

"Nazis," I answered.

"Nazis?"

"Yup. Quite a lot of talk about Nazis."

"See, when I told you not to talk about radios I thought it was also implied that you also shouldn't talk about Nazis."

I then told her about the French apartment, the looted art, and the Emerson.

"So, Nazis and radios?"

"They go together like rama lama ding dong," I sang.

"Ok. What did she say when you told her you owned the looted radio?"

"I didn't tell her."

"You didn't tell her?"

"No."

"Why didn't you tell her?"

"She's going to tell me to give it back," I said.

"Of course she's going to tell you to give it back," she said raising her voice, "it's a looted Nazi radio!"

"But it plays so good," I said.

"You have to tell her" she said.

"I know I do," I replied.

But she had already hung up. Shame, such a great radio.

In the end, although we did not go out again, Linda invited me to the ceremony where the looted artifacts were returned to the heirs. I even flew to New York, bringing the Emerson with me, for the occasion. I'm not sure who I handed the radio to, I think maybe a third cousin, but he acted a little like I had given him a bag of turds. I guess he was hoping for the Renoir.

I wasn't going to replace the Emerson but, soon after the ceremony, I saw one on eBay.

It was in ok condition.

It didn't play.

I bought it anyway.

It came from a seller in Toledo, Ohio. I was pretty sure it hadn't been stolen. But I didn't display it, just in case.

1938 STEWART WARNER SLED

My friend Gili Rosen called.

"I have a radio for you," she said.

This was my favorite kind of phone call. "Really?"

"Yeah, we were cleaning up Carl's cottage and found it in the attic."

Carl was Gili's late father in law.

"Nice," I said, "I'll be right over."

"Don't get your hopes up," she replied, "it has seen better days."

I liked going to Harry and Gili's house because, aside from the promise of free food, they always appeared to be genuinely pleased to see me. I would go in, rummage around the kitchen, ask Nida, who was their housekeeper, when she planned to make me chicken adobo, and generally would make myself feel at home. In return, I would launch into a twenty-minute self-deprecating tirade, replete with references to failed seductions and golf balls going awry and astray. There was not much in life which gave me more pleasure than making the Rosens laugh, and if their sometimes-cynical Gen X son Jacob laughed too, then I would know I was at the top of my game.

When I got there this time, I found the added bonus that Harry's niece, Sarah, her husband Micah, and daughter Elise, were visiting from Israel. Ordinarily, I don't really like guests, or any people for that matter, but Sarah had once worked for me at Tumbleweed Press and she loved to tell the story of how she brought me Tim Hortons coffee instead of Starbucks and I sent her back to get it right. It is a story which I'm sure never happened but she took a lot of pleasure in recounting it and who am I to deprive someone of life's little pleasures - even if it was a total fabrication. In addition, Harry had told me that Elise's favorite book was Crazy for Canada which, although I had not written, was a Tumbleweed book and so, being vain and self-centered, I was heading over there to receive my well-earned accolades.

Elise did indeed love Crazy for Canada and Sarah went on about it and it was all going splendidly until I asked if Harry had given her my latest book - My Afternoon Guest - and Sarah, in very typical Israeli fashion said, "yes, we read it to her. She didn't like it at all."

Which should have been my first clue that dark clouds were ahead. That's when I should have left.

But I still hadn't had my pie.

I was wiping the remnants of the strawberry rhubarb from my chin, eyeing a second piece, when Micah, Sarah's husband, said, "you know, I'm also a little bit in publishing."

This is usually when somebody will tell me they have written this very cute book about a dog with three legs or a cat with five, and how they read the story to their kid and then to the kids at daycare and how everyone said they should publish it and would I mind taking a look at it. And this is usually the time I would stab myself with the knife I would have used to cut myself a piece of pie.

But Micah was actually in publishing. He worked with a publisher in Israel which translated the works of European philosophers into Hebrew.

"Huge market," I joked, although I realized this was a bit rich coming from someone who had only sold 27 copies of his short story collection. Then, catching myself out and also remembering that my friend Allie had told me to be a little less full of myself and ask other people questions, I said, "wow, that is really interesting. Which philosophers?"

Micah, who had a PhD in philosophy, then, foolishly treating me like an equal, rhymed off a series of Germanic sounding names - the majority I was quite sure were made up or medical conditions. I just nodded my head like the idiot I am until he said, "and of course Spinoza."

I was familiar with Spinoza, if only barely, but my insecurity and uneasiness generally cause me to resort to humor, and so I hesitated just a little because I was forming my reply ("of course, shortstop for the 1967 Yankees." Which I think would have been funny), but he pounced on my hesitation and said, "you know who Spinoza is?"

But it was the way he said it.

"You know who Spinoza is?" Do you hear the disdain?

Then Sarah looked at me and, in her face, I could see she was thinking, "I used to get this guy coffee?"

Even Harold seemed a bit disappointed in me. This was not good.

I was usually the guy who made other people feel like shit for being dumb. That was my thing.

Then the baby cried and I slowly slinked out of the house declaring it had been one of the worst nights ever.

Gili yelled out, "You forgot the radio!"

I told her I would come back. Not even a radio could salvage my mood.

When I got home, I ordered Will Durant's Story of Philosophy from Amazon. I also spent about two hours reading up on Spinoza and his mentors and disciples. The book arrived the next day.

I read the first 50 pages.

I mean, I read the words that were on the first 50 pages. They could have, for all intents and purposes, been written in Aramaic.

Nothing was sinking in. Nothing. Not a word.

Jesus.

Was I dumb? Was I that guy?

Can there be anything worse than being really dumb but thinking you were really smart?

Jesus.

I read the 50 pages again. Still nothing.

Maybe Will Durant who had, with his wife, written the ten volume Story of Civilization, was a lousy writer.

Nah.

The guy was a genius. It was me. I was straight-up dumb.

The phone rang. It was my niece Rena. She was coming back from her religion class.

"Have you had an assignment yet?" I asked.

She said they had to go on YouTube and watch a commencement address given by a writer about atheism and write an essay on it.

And I said, "oh, David Foster Wallace."

And she said, "what?"

And I repeated, "David Foster Wallace."

And she said, "how do you know that?" She was completely dumbfounded.

I explained that DFW was one of my favorite writers, and that some of his essays were considered classics in the field.

"It's called This is Water, right?"

"Yesssssss!"

"Yeah. Great commencement speech."

"Wow," she said, "you're smart."

And I said, "well, lucky guess." Because, you know, I'm nothing if not modest. I hung up and thought to myself.

I am smart!

Here I had let this two-bit philosophy charlatan make me doubt myself. David Foster Wallace.

Damn right!

I grabbed my car keys and drove over to the Rosens.

I was going to tell Micah where he could shove his Spinoza. I marched into the house. Gili said, "come back for your radio?"

"Forget about the radio," I replied. "Where's Micah?" Micah was on the couch reading a book to his daughter. I did not hesitate.

"So," I said. "My niece just called."

"Nice," he said.

"Yeah," I stormed on. "She's taking a religion course and had to watch a commencement speech from this writer."

Then Micah, as casually as possible said, "This is Water by David Foster Wallace." Like nothing. Like shaking hands.

And I, more than a little deflated, said, "yeah."

And he said, "nice."

And I said, almost in a whisper, I said, "I knew that."

And Micah, without looking up, turning a page of Crazy for Canada which, to be fair, Elise was really enjoying, said, "Ron, everyone knows that."

The radio was a 1938 Stewart Warner.

A wood radio with a very distinctive art deco design. Collectors called it The Sled. Gili was wrong about the shape. It was actually a beauty. I plugged it in and, although not the greatest sound, this original unrestored 1938 radio was playing really nicely. I wish I had known that Carl had it while he was alive. I carried it to my car and placed it carefully on the floor of the front passenger seat.

Then I went back into the house and got myself a piece of pie. Because, you know, I may be dumb, but I'm not that dumb.

1940 EMERSON PATRIOT CATALIN

One Saturday in July, in the year 1972, Susan Edmonds and her family had a garage sale. I was thirteen years old.

I know it was July because it was a very hot day and I know it was a Saturday because I had fought with my father in the morning about not wanting to go to synagogue. The Edmonds' garage sale, they had signs posted on nearly all of the trees of our street, Place des Pins, in Dollard des Ormeaux, a suburb of Montreal, was scheduled between 9am and noon. It was the exact time of the Saturday morning service at the Beth Tikvah Synagogue. The Edmondses were not Jewish so it is unlikely that Mrs. Edmonds turned to Mr. Edmonds and said, "Honey, maybe we should start after the Haftorah."

I know it was 1972 because I had had my bar mitzvah in May and I had money. This story is a little bit about money and the only time I had money was after my bar mitzvah. Most of the gifts were in the form of savings bonds but a couple of envelopes contained cold hard cash.

Anyway, with my bar mitzvah now over I really didn't see the point of going to synagogue, but my father didn't see it that way. The Zevys did not go to or have garage sales so I could not use that as an excuse, so instead I told my father I was going to go see Stevie Sheen's grandmother in the hospital.

Now neither my father nor I for that matter knew whether Stevie Sheen even had a grandmother, but my father figured that if I wanted something bad enough to invent a sick grandmother, then maybe he should pick his fights.

What I wanted, or thought I wanted, was Susan Edmonds.

Stevie Sheen and I decided that the way to Susan Edmonds' heart was through the junk her family had decided to sell.

It was, we thought, a very solid plan.

I would like to say that in the fifty years since I have hatched better plans with which to attract women. But I'm not sure I have.

Of course, I can't speak about Stevie Sheen.

Although neither Stevie nor I could be considered anything close to cool, we knew enough not to arrive right at 9:00am, so we rode our bikes over at 9:45 and, in a moment of sheer audacity, decided to drive right by a few times as if we had been just out for a bike ride when some vintage item caught our eyes.

Which would have been a very good plan had the Edmonds' garage sale been an actual garage sale and not a sale of hand-me-down clothes previously worn by Susan Edmonds and her two sisters.

And so, Stevie and I were the only boys there. In retrospect, I realize we had hit the jackpot but at the time, I could only feel shame and embarrassment.

We stood there in frozen animation until Mrs. Edmonds said, "boys, if you hurry you can catch Musof." No, she didn't say that.

What she said was, "Suzie look. Your little friends are here. Go get them a glass of lemonade."

So, we stood there like the schmucks we were until Mr. Edmonds said, "boys, I wasn't going to sell her, what with all this frou frou girls' stuff, but if I get enough for it, I might part with my Emerson Patriot. Now just hold on while I go get it."

Mr. Edmonds was only gone for about ten minutes but, although we didn't speak, for those ten minutes I'm pretty sure both Stevie and I thought we were about to buy a dog.

My mother was going to kill me.

But an Emerson Patriot was, thankfully, not a dog, it was, or so Mr. Edmonds said, a radio.

"Now she doesn't work, but I'm sure all she needs is a couple of new capacitors and tubes and you'll have her humming. You'll be listening to the Expos in no time. Forty bucks and she's all yours."

I took out my wallet and gave Mr. Edmonds, with Susan Edmonds nowhere in sight, forty dollars, and Stevie and I sheepishly walked back to our bikes. I couldn't ride with a broken-down Emerson in my hands, so Stevie rode next to me while I carried the radio in one arm and pushed my bike with the other.

Now Stevie, who had only the day prior helped me fix the chain on my bike, knew I didn't know what a capacitor or tube was. He also knew I couldn't walk into my house with a broken-down table radio.

He also didn't have forty dollars.

So, he traded me three baseball cards for it. Maury Wills, Rusty Staub, and John Bocabella.

Mr. Sheen got the radio working in less time than Stevie took to fix the chain on my bike. We listened to a few Expos games on it in the backyard while playing catch.

Sound was pretty good but we both preferred our nifty transistor radios. I think Stevie felt he got the worst of the deal.

The Rusty Staub was a rookie card.

By the time the Sheens moved a few years later, the radio had stopped working, and it ended up on the curb for the garbageman.

Last year I bought one from a dealer in Miami. It was more than forty dollars.

I told the dealer it had sentimental value. "Is that right," she said. "How so?"

"I actually owned one in 1972."

I didn't tell her I only owned it for fifteen minutes. There are some things you just have to keep to yourself.

1940 BANG AND OLUFSEN 40 'BEOLIT'

Every once in a while, someone will try to fix me up with another man. Now, this is not because I am 63, and have never been married. It is because I play golf.

This always ends up being someone's uncle or father or grandfather who, like me, spends the winter in Florida. Nothing could interest me less than spending four hours with a complete stranger and that is usually what I tell them. They will ordinarily counter with, "I think you two would get along." I then explain that I do not want to get along. I have more than my share of golf partners.

There are however, a handful of people in my life to whom I cannot say no. One is my dear friend Dani who, along with being my close friend, was also the first employee at Tumbleweed. She began her email by saying 'please, please, please don't feel under any obligation to say yes.'

Which, right away, means there is no chance I can say no.

The email continues with 'my sister's rabbi is coming to Florida...' I then maybe passed out.

When I came to, the gist of the favor was that the rabbi was coming to Florida and he loved golf and could I maybe play golf with him. And then something about how nice he was with one of the kid's bar mitzvah or something, and 'really, feel free to say no,' and 'the only reason I am even considering it is that his parents were from Egypt and you might get a good story out of it.'

His name was Rabbi Dan. Rabbi Dan.

'It would be my pleasure,' I said.

'It's ok if it's only 9 holes,' Dani said.

18 was never an option. But I didn't tell her that. The rabbi had a slice. A bad slice.

We had only played three holes and he had already hit two houses.

Aside from when I play with my brother, I don't give any unsolicited advice or instruction on the golf course. I don't like to get it, and I live by the rule of treat someone like you want to be treated.

If the Rabbi was my brother, I might have said, 'listen rabbi, maybe you want to line up facing a little left because all your shots are going to the right and maybe you want to compensate a little.'

But he was not my brother. He was Rabbi Dan.

So, I said nothing.

I did have what I thought was a pretty good joke about how you are only supposed to lean right on Passover but, although I thought it was funny, I didn't really know Rabbi Dan well enough to be telling this type of joke.

Also, I wasn't entirely sure if you were supposed to lean right or to lean left. So, I said nothing.

Rabbi Dan, dressed in golf attire, his new Boca Grove golf cap covering his kippah, did not look like a rabbi. He looked like a golfer. Albeit a bad one.

My brother-in-law, who is, I think, more orthodox than Rabbi Dan, once went kayaking at the cottage in the white shirt and black pants, and his long beard, which are the traditional garb of the orthodox Jew. Although he was a very good kayaker, he still looked like an Orthodox Jew. Had another Jewish kayaker come across him on the lake on that Sunday morning, he might have felt compelled to wish him a good week, a shavuah tov, which is the common greeting.

Rabbi Dan was clean shaven, and aside from the fact that he played like someone who spent the majority of his hours conducting his rabbinical duties instead of, say, going to the driving range and trying to fix his slice, there was nothing about him that made him look like a rabbi.

Despite not being very good, he was having a wonderful time, and since we spent the first nine holes only talking about golf and he didn't once ask me why I didn't go to synagogue, I decided we would play 18 holes. He didn't thank me for playing 18 holes because that is what he assumed, and it is a fair assumption when one is invited to play golf, but I had a page full of 'I can only play 9' excuses.

None of which I had to use.

I say we played 18, but in truth, we only played 17 because my house backs into 17 and I suggested we stop there and grab a beer. Sometimes my guests are not too thrilled about stopping one hole early - often because they are keeping score so they want to finish the course. Which always irritates me because it is not as if, without exception, they are on their way to shooting the best round of their life which is, to me, really the only reason to play 18, because you know, my house is right there.

I said this to Rabbi Dan after he quickly and readily accepted my offer for a beer and then, since Rabbi Dan had, in addition to a bad slice, a pretty good sense of humor, he asked what the record for the number of houses hit in a round was. I laughed and said he was close but not that close and besides, number 18 doesn't have any houses.

We took a picture of ourselves on the green of number 17 and I sent it to Dani.

It had been a relatively painless, if pressed, I might even say enjoyable afternoon and, I'm not sure if Hashem grants extra points for playing golf with a rabbi, but if he does, and if he is a fair almighty, I think there should be extra points for playing with a rabbi who has a bad slice.

But I wasn't in this for the points, for Dani or Hashem. I'm just saying.

Rabbi Dan downed his beer in nearly one gulp. Pretty impressive for a clergyman.

He made appropriate remarks about my radio collection - impressed but not overly effusive.

I prefer overly effusive but I'm guessing this was a Rabbi thing. He can't play favorites with his congregants.

He thanked me again and was about to leave, when he spotted the 1940 Bang and Olufsen Beolit perched on the top shelf of my display in the living room.

"We had that radio in our house in Cleveland growing up," he said. "My father, alav ha shalom, schlepped it all the way from Cairo."

This was the first time either of us had mentioned that we had parents who were from Egypt.

It seemed a little weird, to me at least, that Rabbi Dan had drunk his beer, wandered around my collection, and not once mentioned

- which is the default statement of people when they see my radios - that he too grew up with a vintage radio.

I went to the bathroom and when I came back, he handed me his phone. In my short absence he had found a family photo. Sure enough, there was Rabbi Dan's family posing around the radio.

It was a nice example of that model. Unlike mine, where half of one of the four front nobs is missing. "You still have it?" I asked.

"Unfortunately not, got lost in one of our moves."

"Shame," I said. "Would you mind sending me that photo? If it's ok, I'll add it to my website."

"My pleasure," he said.

"Must have been his pride and joy for him to have brought it all this way with him," I said.

Then Rabbi Dan said something which really, really surprised me.

"Not really," he replied, "it was a radio which he kept to remind him of his shame."

"Shame?"

"Yes."

We both stood there in silence. Me, waiting. Then Rabbi Dan said, "this will cost you another beer. If you have the time."

I had the time.

Rabbi Dan took a long pull of his second beer. Then he burped in a very unclerical fashion.

"I'm going to guess that the date Nov 29, 1947 means something to you."

It did. It was the date the United Nations voted on the Palestine partition plan. It was the day that made Herzl's dream real. For me, it was a holy day. Along with May 14, 1948, it was one of my two holy days on the calendar.

"Partition vote," I said.

"My grandfather was in textiles. Import and export. He had a big supplier in the UK. The supplier sent him a Danish radio during the war. It was a token of friendship. Because of how the Danes treated the Jews. He knew my grandfather would appreciate it."

"But that's a lovely story," I said, "why the shame?"

"That comes later. Listen, you maybe have something to nosh on?" I brought him some peanuts.

"And so?"

"The radio became the focal point of the living room. It was, it is," he pointed at my radio, "an absolutely beautiful radio. It also became the focal point of the neighborhood. My father and his friends would gather around listening to the BBC. Then, when the broadcast was over, they would switch the channel back to Egyptian music."

"Umm Kulthum," I said, naming the venerable Egyptian singer and only one I knew.

"Yes," he said, helping himself to a handful of peanuts. "On Nov 29th, he and his regular crew gathered around to listen to the results of the voting. The assembly had tried to vote a few days before but there was going to be another vote. The Zionist contingent were twisting more arms."

I knew the story well. Some of the tales - like the Jewish pineapple king influencing Latin American votes - were legendary. Some were apocryphal. And some were fabrications. It didn't matter. It was an easy win. In our family, my father had pounded the names of countries and how they voted, into our heads. 33 for, 13 against, 10 abstentions. Haiti was good. India was bad.

"It worked," I said.

"Baruch Hashem, praised be God," he replied. Ok. Now he sounded like a rabbi.

"So what was the problem?"

"My father, alav ha shalom, may he rest in peace, was hoping the No vote would win. He was recently married, with a baby on the way. He had joined the family business and was doing well. The Egyptian representative to the UN, along with other Arab delegates, vowed that Jewish blood would flow in retribution. My father wanted the status quo. Did not want to rock the boat. Our family had survived and even prospered in Egypt for generations."

"He was not wrong," I said gently. "If anything, he was prescient."

"Yes, my family lost it all. In the end, with no business and no prospect of jobs and constant anti-Semitism, they left after the 1956 war."

"Mine too. Where did they go?"

"Israel. Via Rome."

"Mine too," I said.

"Then Cleveland."

"And he brought the radio with him?"

"Everywhere. To remind him of that moment."

"I don't think it is anything to be ashamed of," I said.

"Me neither," said Rabbi Dan, "but it was a good reminder. Of what he had. But also, of what he didn't have."

I nodded. I wish I knew where my father, where my uncle, had listened to the news. Had they been scared and worried of the results? Had they danced in the streets? I don't know. I don't think there is anyone left to ask. In 1952 there were assurances from Nasser and his henchmen that the Jews would be safe.

But the assurances were short lived.

The rabbi shook my hand and made his way to the door.

"I'm back in six weeks," he said, "I'll give you a call to see if you want to play."

"It would be my pleasure," I replied.

But it was one call I was going to screen. Rabbi Dan had a really bad slice.

1945 EKCO A-22

There is a lizard in my bathtub.

I am in the bathroom having my pre-afternoon golf pee, when, out of the corner of my eye, I see something moving in the tub.

I'm not crazy about distractions when I have a good stream going, and definitely not crazy about anything moving in my bathtub.

I go investigate.

It is a lizard.

It is not the tiny lizard from the insurance company commercials. This is no gecko. This is a prehistoric reptile about 18 inches long. With a tail twice that size.

It appears to be dead. At least, it is not moving.

So, I of course do what most people do when they encounter a lizard in their bathtub: I get my phone and take a picture.

I take a picture because I know this will be a fantastic gift for my friend Allie. Now Allie is difficult to shop for and whenever I come across a potential gift, I nab it as quick as I can. Lest you think that Allie has a proclivity for reptiles, I should explain that Allie is forever lecturing me about closing doors. The door to my backyard. My front door. My garage door.

"Something is going to get in," she warns.

"What could possibly get in?" I reply.

So now I can give her this exquisite 'I told you so' gift. I text her the picture.

I then go to the pool and get my pool scooper. I'm sure it has another name, but I don't know what else to call it. I go back to the bathroom.

The lizard hasn't moved.

I prod it with the scooper.

And then it moves.

Scares the shit out of me.

It tries to climb out of the tub but it is a very deep tub and the porcelain is very slippery. So, it keeps slipping down.

It would be funny if it weren't so disgusting. I beat a hasty retreat. Allie texts back.

'Oh gross. What is that?' She asks.

'A lizard,' I reply.

'In your bathtub?'

'Yes.'

'How did it get in your bathtub?'

'I don't know.'

'How many times have I told you to close your doors!!'

See? The perfect gift.

'Is it dead?'

'No. But it can't get out.'

Allie knows better than to think I am going to do anything about the lizard.

'What are you going to do?'

'What do you think I'm going to do?'

'You are going to call Lewberg.'

'Of course I'm going to call Lewberg.'

Lewberg wants to know where I am. We are teeing off in five minutes.

I tell him there is a lizard in my bathtub.

He tells me to call security. Without missing a beat. As if I call him every day about a lizard in my bathtub. "They will take care of it."

He tells me to hurry my ass. He doesn't want to play behind this foursome of women.

I close the bathroom doors and call security.

I speak to Freddie.

"There is a lizard in my bathtub," I tell Freddie. Freddie is unfazed.

I'm guessing he has heard it all.

I give him my address and tell him I am leaving the front door unlocked. I also tell him I am leaving $20 for him on the dining room table.

He says he will be right over.

I go play golf with Lewberg and Goldfarb.

I play pretty well considering there is a lizard in my bathtub.

Goldfarb doesn't understand how I can leave the front door unlocked. He has a world class security system. I tell him there's nothing to steal. Besides, I know Freddie.

He says that I have thousands of dollars' worth of radios.

And I say, "believe me, Freddie is welcome to them. They are the bane of my existence."

Then Lewberg says, "nobody ever says 'bane' without 'of my existence.' You ever notice that?"

Every once in a while, Lewberg comes up with a beauty.

"What about your echocardiogram?" Goldfarb asks. "You said it was one of a kind."

That is what Goldfarb calls my EKCO A22. He says when I talk about it, he can see my heart racing.

The 1945 British-made EKCO 22 might be the prize of my collection. I have managed to snag myself a very hard to find working model.

"Yes," I agree reluctantly, "it is pretty rare."

"There you go," he says. "Just lock your door." He might have a point.

After golf, I gingerly open the bathroom door. No lizard.

Good old Freddie.

The phone rings.

It is Freddie.

And this is what he says. He says, "I'm on my way."

As he says that, I walk with my phone to the dining room. The $20 is still on the table.

I say, "Freddie, you haven't been here yet?"

"No man, baby gator at the Shapiros'. We just got it out. I'll be there in five."

He hangs up before I can tell him the lizard is gone.

I look in the tub. There is a scrape in the porcelain. An actual scrape.

So now there's a lizard running around my house. I text Allie. She says she wants to throw up.

She says do I want to sleep at her place tonight. Then she says, 'I told you so.'

I'm good for three or four birthdays.

I show Freddie the scrape.

And Freddie says, "well I'll be damned."

Then he says, "you always leave your back door open like that?"

Freddie does a cursory search of the house and gives me his cell phone number.

"Call me if it turns up."

I give him the $20.

Now I'm not scared of no lizard.

But if I want to lock myself in my bedroom all night, not even going to the kitchen for my nightly bowl of Cheerios, then that is my right.

Has nothing to do with a lizard on the prowl.

Of course, if you are going to lock yourself in your room, you had better make sure you haven't locked yourself in with a recently escaped reptile.

My curtains move.

And there is no wind.

Maybe I stand on my bed for a minute or two. Then I summon the courage to go take a look.

Yup.

Lizard at three o'clock.

I text Freddie.

I tell him the front door is unlocked.

Freddie is here five minutes later. He corners the lizard, grabs it by the tail, dangles it out of the room, with me trailing safely ten feet behind, then flings it out the front door.

Now I don't want to throw any shade on Freddie. Guy came right over. Showed no fear.

Grabbed the lizard like it was nothing.

The thing is.

Freddie is not a world class lizard flinger.

You see, you want to release at the apex. But Freddie. Well Freddie releases early. Very early.

So, the lizard, instead of being flung across my front yard, lands on my porch, a yard or two from where Freddie and I are standing. The lizard then promptly gets up on its two hind legs and, my hand to god, runs right back into my house.

And then Freddie says, "well I'll be damned." We search the house. No lizard.

Freddie says I should text him if it shows up. I give him another $20.

Somehow, I manage to sleep.

The next day, Emma and her cleaning crew arrive. Emma lectures me about closing doors.

I say, "yes, I'm going to close doors."

I'm pretty sure the lizard is gone. Until I see it in the kitchen.

Then, I'm not that sure any more.

Emma, Indiana and Rosita then team up to shoo the frightened to death lizard out of the house, into the backyard, and then out of the backyard onto the 17th fairway.

They aren't about to let no diablo lizard mess up their clean house.

And that is that.

Lesson learned.

Or so I think.

Goldfarb decides that two days of lizard hell is not enough of a lesson.

Learning to shut the door is one thing. But he is going to teach me to lock my door.

And so, that night, while Lewberg and I are out at dinner, Goldfarb lets himself into my unlocked door in order to steal my prized EKCO radio.

I know this because when I get home, although there is no lizard in my bathtub, there is a Goldfarb on my living room floor.

"Oh, my back," he wails in pain, "my fucking back."

Goldfarb threw out his trick back while trying to pick up the radio.

See, Goldfarb knows the 1945 EKCO A-22 is really, really rare. What he didn't know, is that it is also really, really heavy.

"Goldfarb," I say while helping him up, "how many times have I told you that you have to lift with your knees!"

1945 FADA BULLET

For a while, every time I received a new radio, I would take a photograph and post it on our family group chat. Pretty soon after posting Daniel, my niece's boyfriend, would then post a thumbs up emoji. My niece Sammy, who has two kids, reads her correspondence late at night, and would sometimes write 'whoa cool.' Most of the rest of the family would just ignore me.

That's ok.

Everybody has lives and radios are my thing. And so, when I post a photo of a 1939 Fada Bullet, one of the kids might say nice. But often, my pic is supplanted by adorable pictures and videos of Jojo and baby Lou Lou. Pictures and videos which I find adorable too. So, I don't get into the whole thing about how one of the people I have bought transistors from told me about this estate sale in Athens, Georgia. Turns out they had this Fada Bullet which the owner had meticulously and painstakingly returned to its original 1945 alabaster color. That all the gorgeous burnt orange catalins were almost all originally alabaster. That the previous owner had stipulated in his will that the radio could not be shipped. That it had to be picked up locally. I'm not going to interrupt the chat after the super cute video of Joey singing 'happy birthday Bubby' by telling everyone that I drove to Athens, Georgia to pick up a radio. And was not on a golf trip with my friend Phil. They all think I'm crazy enough as it is.

I am still in the honeymoon phase of collecting and that means I want to share my joy with everyone.

Whether they are interested or not.

Dave is the name of my postal carrier. He carries the boxes of radios from his truck to my front door. If I am home, right into my house. I have invited him in so he can see what he has been schlepping. The FedEx guy and UPS guy too. Last night, the UberEATS driver, after exclaiming, "cool collection dude," was invited in for a short tour while my veggie lo mein got cold.

If there is a break in, there will be a long list of suspects.

That's on me.

I am proud of my collection and, to be perfectly honest, more than a little envious of others. There is a couple in Nebraska whose house is nothing short of being a catalin museum. They own an example, in each color, of virtually every catalin radio ever made.

Unlike me, the majority of collectors are private in nature. Some have written books. But the majority just collect and keep to themselves.

As I started to amass numbers I decided, just out of curiosity, to look up what the Guinness World Record was for number of radios. I'm quite sure that the Guinness Book of World Records is no longer a thing. Certainly not like it was back in the day.

I was more than a little surprised by what I found. An M. Prakash of India held the record for having 625 different types of radio. The record, not unlike Bob Beamon's long jump record, had been in the books since 2005.

When I mentioned this record to one of the dealers I buy from she laughed and laughed. I only wish one of my stories could get a laugh like that. She said she knew collectors who had over 2000 radios. But why don't they submit it to Guinness I asked. Then she gave me the kind of look that people give you when they think you're crazy.

Ok.

I wasn't really that serious anyway but I was still a little curious about the wording of the record. To me, it sounded a little ambiguous.

625 different types of radios. Did that include transistors?

What about the same radio but in a different color? Was that a different type?

So, I sent an email off to the good folk at Guinness. Their website said expect 6-18 months for a response.

So that was that.

Anyway, I didn't have enough shelves.

This honeymoon phase was affecting a judgment which was already teetering on the edge of sanity. I started giving away radios to anyone who expressed an interest.

And to many who did not.

My bankers. My tailors. My candlestick makers.

Part of my rational was sentimental and not completely loony - a part of me would be in my friends' and families' homes.

Honestly, I thought that was kind of nice.

The other part was based on a shakier foundation: if, I thought, instead of giving a radio away, I was actually just lending it on a permanent loan, then the radios I gave away, would still be in my collection. I would give a radio in exchange for a shelf.

It was, I thought, nothing short of brilliant.

Ok, M. Prakash of India or his heirs still didn't have much to worry about but at least I had a number to shoot for.

It was, I foolishly convinced myself, win-win.

Also, there actually were quite a number of radios I had purchased in the early days which I was quite happy to get rid of to make room for better radios.

Win-win.

So, like the arriviste I am, don't look it up, it's not a good quality to have, I updated my website and added a Courtesy of the Rosen (or whatever family name) Collection next to the radios I had given away. Which is what somebody might have in a coffee table book if they had photos of other people's radios.

But I was just being a self-centered fool.

It only took me two weeks to realize I was being a self-centered fool. Which is, as you might have guessed, a personal record. I then deleted all the radios which were not mine. No more 'courtesy of'. A radio was either mine or not. You can't have it both ways.

Now while two weeks is frankly a pretty decent amount of time to discover a modicum of self-awareness, it was still enough time to cause some damage.

That's on me.

I should have known better than to have put my eggs into the basket of a sleep-deprived, workaholic mother of a newborn. One, the mother, not the newborn, who had just bought a new house.

I'm not going to name names but this woman, along with being a fan of my writing, absolutely loved my radios. She thought they were the coolest thing.

I urged her to pick one.

She couldn't.

I explained about the permanent loan and M. Prakash in India.

She said really?

I said yeah. It would be my pleasure.

And she said ok, how do I choose.

I said, I will send you my website. You can choose any radio that has a Canadian flag next to it.

She said really?

I said yeah. Take anything you want.

She said I'm so excited.

And I said great.

Then two days went by and she didn't get back to me. So, I sent her an email with my website again.

Then again. And then, again.

Newborn. New house. Busy job. Maybe a little more on her mind than choosing one of my precious radios.

I get that.

Listen.

I'm not an idiot.

So, of course, I sent another reminder.

I mean, I really wanted her to get a radio.

She answered that night.

Actually, the time stamp on the email said 3am.

'Sorry for taking so long. Things have been hectic. Thank you so much for your generosity. Saul and I really appreciate it. It means so much to us. We just spent an hour on your website and this is the one we absolutely love. Thank you so much.'

And she included a picture of the radio. With a whole bunch of heart emojis.

Now the reason I put a Canadian flag next to some of the radios is just a function of inventory control. Which are in Toronto. And which are in Florida. I have people only look for the radios in Toronto because then they can pick them up or I can drop them off. Much easier than shipping from Florida.

Also, and I would like to put this as delicately as I can, even though I have fantastic radios in Canada, I mean some real beauties, all of the rare hard to find catalin radios are in Florida.

So, I can, you know, be a real macher. A real big shot. Sure, take anything you want.

So now I have pestered this sleep deprived mother of a newborn for two weeks.

Have you picked a radio yet?

Am I now supposed to say - hey, I don't think that radio has a Canadian flag next to it.

I mean. Maybe I'm a dick. But not that big of a dick.

So I shipped her the 1945 Fada Catalin Bullet from Florida.

The one I had driven to Athens, Georgia for.

The one in mint shape.

The one that still played.

They've got it displayed really nicely in the living room.

It's a centerpiece.

"The baby loves to turn it off and on," she said beaming. "Isn't that cute?"

"Yes," I replied, discreetly wiping what I believed was mashed apricots from the 83-year-old grill. In another 83 or so years, the alabaster would turn into the same color as those apricots.

"Yes," I said. "That's really cute."

1946 CYARTS

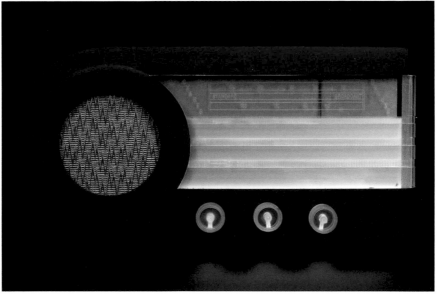

With permission of Decophobia

There was this pawnshop Goldfarb liked to go to in Miami. It was owned by a French Canadian who had moved to Florida after retiring from his job at the Molson's beer plant. This man, Daniel Lafleur, was his name, lasted about three weeks doing nothing on the beach. And so, fulfilling a lifelong dream, bought himself a pawnshop from a Cuban man whose lifelong dream was to do nothing on a beach. Goldfarb came across the pawnshop, which had the very un-pawnshop-like 'The Flower Pawnshop', because it was a block away from a place where he bought Dominican cigars that he then passed off as Cubans to the starters at our golf course. Goldfarb had this whole scam going and both Lewberg and I benefitted from it because we played most of our rounds with Goldfarb who now got very preferential treatment.

Goldfarb rarely bought anything, but the pawnshop was a reality show in real life and he was fascinated by the characters who staggered into the store with what were likely ill-gotten wares. Goldfarb talked about hockey and all things Montreal with Lafleur and was not surprised to learn that what he missed most were the smoked meat sandwiches from Schwartz's on boulevard Saint-Laurent. Goldfarb too was an aficionado of the cured meat and the next time he went to the store, he brought Lafleur a sandwich from Schwartzman's - which was a deli in Boca, fifteen minutes from our club, which had brazenly named itself in a manner that implied it was affiliated with the venerable Montreal charcuterie. Which was not very kosher but it turned out the smoked meat was nearly just as good.

Lafleur was thrilled and, in return, he let Goldfarb anchor himself in the store for an hour or so and once, even let him behind the counter while Lafleur tended to an errand.

Goldfarb would then come back and regale Lewberg and I with tales of misfits, ne'er do wells, and desperados.

It wasn't schadenfreude, but Goldfarb did seem to take a little of perverse pleasure in hearing and seeing other people's woes and misery. It was all frankly a little sad but Goldfarb brought us smoked meat sandwiches too so it was a small price to pay.

One day, while about to tee off on number 7, Goldfarb turned to me and said, "the Flower got a radio today."

I striped my drive down the driveway and then turned to him and asked, "really? Do you know what kind?"

Goldfarb then stepped up to the tee, hit his drive over the fence and nearly onto the Turnpike, declared he was taking a mulligan, and then said, "nope."

"Well, can you describe it," I asked, "was it wood?"

"It was a radio," he said poking his club at the bushes in the left side of the fairway.

"Goldfarb," Lewberg said, "your ball went way over." He pointed to the Florida Turnpike.

Lewberg and I then waited in the fairway while Goldfarb, having squeezed his ample body through a crack in the bushes, foraged the long grass, steps from the bustling highway, looking for his ball. As usual, his ball did not emerge but he retrieved seven others to take its place.

Now cheered up by his new bounty, he became a little more talkative.

"It was blue," he said.

"Painted?" I asked.

"How the hell should I know?" he exclaimed. On 14, Goldfarb fished four balls out of the pond.

He was cleaning them off when he said, "I took a picture."

And I said, "what?"

Goldfarb said "I took a picture. Sorry I completely forgot." He grabbed his phone from the cart, scrolled through his album, and handed me the phone.

I recognized it right away.
It was the 1946 Cyarts.
In blue.

When I first started collecting radios, I created a wish list. The Cyarts was on the top of list.

It was manufactured with unusual materials - Plexon and Lucite.

It was bullet-shaped. Because of the translucent Lucite, the radio was absolutely stunning when lit up.

I had never seen one.

Had never even heard of someone having one. Decophobia had 4 in their sold radio data base but had a huge waiting list for the next one.

In time, I removed it from my wish list.

It was like having Mila Kunis on your wish list.

Goldfarb and I drove down to Miami after golf. Lafleur said he wanted $200 for it.

Goldfarb, who had been a proverbial fly on the wall at hundreds of negotiations, said, "we won't give you a dollar more than $100."

Lafleur countered with $175.

Goldfarb shook his head and said, "it's not even wood. Made of cheap plastic. Probably made in Hong Kong."

We settled on $166.

In the car I said, "it's stolen right."

And Goldfarb, barely able to contain his glee said, "oh yeah."

The radio sang like a siren. And all lit up? Well, all lit up, it looked like a heavenly beacon.

Now I'm not sure what the Florida law is and I only have a vague understanding of Talmudic law but I knew I had to do the right thing. Now the right thing was to call the police and tell them I had just acquired a rare Cyarts radio from a pawn shop in Miami which I was pretty sure, the radio not the pawn shop, had been stolen.

Which is what I did.

It took me several tries and a long hold period before I got to the right person. I'm guessing the Miami police department has more pressing issues than missing old radios, even those that lit up, because the person on the other line did not show a lot of interest and I was pretty sure she wasn't writing anything down.

Of course, when she said, "a blue 1976 cyborg," I just said, "yes," because, you know, there's the right thing, and then there's the smart thing.

But, in order to have a completely clean conscience, I also added a note next to the picture of the Cyarts on my website.

'Bought at pawnshop in Miami. Please contact with proof if this was stolen from you.'

Now, to say my website does not get much traffic is a little like saying I don't make many eagles and so I figured I was in the clear. But a week later I received an email with a picture of the blue Cyarts with a note saying he was a Miami collector and the Cyarts, along with a few other rare radios, had recently been stolen. He included a copy of the police report. He lived a few blocks from the pawn shop so it all made sense and the next time Goldfarb went down to Miami, he brought the radio and dropped it off.

So that was that.

I didn't have the Cyarts or Mila Kunis but I had done the right thing.

Which is something, I guess.

I also had a pretty good story. The story you are reading now.

So, I typed it up in all of its glory and send it along with the photos of the Cyarts to Helen, who lays out the stories and designs the books.

In addition to being a great designer, Helen is a good friend and she is always quick to compliment my work. This time was no exception and she said 'Great story!' which was very nice but then she sent me another email. And in that email, she said, 'I don't think it's the same radio'

She then attached a bunch of photos and had circled the areas in the photo I had originally on my website with the one the guy who said it had been stolen sent me and, even I, who did not have the greatest eye for detail, could see it was not the exact same radio.

'Could it be the light or the angle the picture was taken?' I asked.

'No,' she replied, 'they are two different radios.'

Then I said, 'Hold the presses.'

No, I didn't really say that.

One of the security guards at our gate is a former police officer. She is way too classy for donuts so I usually bring her croissants. I brought her the copy of the police report and she laughed in my face.

I said, "not real."

And she said, "no, Honey. Not even close. Thanks for the croissant."

Now I knew what the right thing to do was but that had not really served me all that well. Instead, Goldfarb and I decided to do the wrong thing.

Now, I can't really get into too much detail because we may have broken a law or two, but the wrong thing was going back to the pawn shop, asking Mr. Lafleur to let us know the next time the guy who had pawned the radio to him came in, contact the guy, who was very proficient in relieving people of their possessions, and... well, I can't really say much more. Only that Goldfarb knew where the scammer lived and let's just say he didn't have great security at his house.

I don't have the radio on my website any more.

But, if you drive by my house one evening, you can see it shining brightly in the window.

And if you listen hard, you can hear it singing its siren song.

1947 NORTHERN ELECTRIC BABY CHAMP

In the fall of 1977 I drove from Montreal to Toronto in my father's hand-me-down Chevy Impala in order to start my first year of university.

The car was given to me with the very small caveat that its maiden voyage would also include the body and possessions of a woman by the name of Isabelle Goldberg. The body was very much alive but we had not driven very far before I wished it were not. Isabelle was the daughter of a woman my mother played cards with. We were, Isabelle and I, not her mother, the same age but did not run in the same circles. Isabelle had, since our paths would cross from time to time, made it clear that she thought my circles were a little too square.

Which was fair enough.

Isabelle was going to Toronto to attend OCA - the Ontario College of Art. My friend Bernie Good would say she was more than a little artsy-fartsy. It was hard to disagree.

But Isabelle needed a ride and my mother needed a card partner so it came to be that I went, in the opposite direction of Toronto mind you, to pick her up at her parents' tony house in TMR.

Isabelle was waiting for me at the curb. By her side were Mr. and Mrs. Goldberg, two large Samsonite suitcases, a suit bag, a small duffle bag, and 8 red plastic milk crates filled with what appeared to be her entire record collection. These milk crates were the perfect size and shape for record albums, and I'm quite sure every teen in the 70s used them to store their records.

Now I'm not entirely sure what I said when I saw these 8 milk crates but I'm going to guess that since Mr. and Mrs. Goldberg were standing right there I did not say, "are you kidding me!" It is more likely that I said, "I'm not sure those are going to fit." Or something along those lines. Mr. Goldberg said, "oh, it will fit," with the determination of someone who was sure as hell going to get those 8 milk crates of records out of his house.

I'm not sure how, but Mr. Goldberg and I managed to squeeze everything in, although I had to eventually decide to relinquish the spare tire in order to make more room, with Isabelle really sealing her fate by stating, "I've never even heard of anyone getting a flat tire."

I guess not in TMR.

At some point I am going to have to come clean and say that those 8 milk crates contained what could have been the finest collection of Jazz and Blues albums - I think she had all of the Blue Note label - ever amassed: one that today I would likely give my proverbial left arm for. But, at the time, I was living on a steady diet of Frampton Comes Alive and Bob Seger and did not know the difference between Sonny Rollins and Sonny McGee.

Like I said, Mr. Goldberg and I got everything in and they all said their goodbyes with interminable hugs and accompanying tears - it was Toronto, not the Vietnam War - and we were all ready to go when Isabelle shrieked, "wait, I forgot Poppy's radio."

Poppy, it turned out, was Mrs. Goldberg's father. Isabelle ran into the house and came back cradling, no joke, a pink baby blanket, which was wrapped around what was presumably Poppy's radio.

The trunk and back seat were already teeming with her possessions - I could not see out the rear-view mirror, and so, after a little bit of hemming and quite a lot of hawing, I resignedly tucked the pink blanket-covered radio next to my feet on the floor. Not exactly safe but it was too late for that now.

The fight began before we got to the Décarie Expressway. It started, as you might imagine, rather innocuously. "You have a lot of records," I said.

And she said "Thanks." Although I had not exactly meant it as a compliment.

"You had to take them all?" This is me clarifying the ambiguity.

"I just never know what I will be in the mood for," she countered. "Could be Getz, could be Ellington, it could be Miles."

"Jazz, eh?" I said.

"The salve of all wounds," she replied. "I couldn't imagine living without it."

Then I said, "I dunno, doesn't it all kinda sound the same?"

Now, she could have laughed. Because, although I wasn't entirely joking, we both knew I was. She instead swiveled 90 degrees in her seat, looked directly at me and said "Well, what kind of music do you like?"

My answer was a lie. But I knew it would piss her off. "I really like disco," I replied with a straight face.

And then it got a little ugly. Names were called. Lineages were questioned. Neither of us wanting to relent. At one point I might have said, "who the hell says salve!!"

Then, we did not speak for four hours.

Not true.

Twice Isabelle turned to me and quietly said, "I have to pee."

Here's the other thing I'm going to come clean about. I knew the radio was lying on the floor on the driver's side. Knew it when I unloaded her Samsonite suitcases, her suit bag. Knew it when I unloaded her small duffle and knew it when I unloaded all 8 of the milk crates.

I knew it the entire time. But didn't say anything.

My roommate, and soon to become lifelong friend, David Hoffman, said, "should I be concerned that you brought a pink baby blanket, or worse, a baby?"

I shrugged my shoulders and said, "my grandpa's radio. Has sentimental value."

Then I unwrapped it and saw the 1947 Northern Electric with its classic art deco design and four tube chassis for the first time.

"She's a beauty," said David, "does it work?"

"Damn straight!" I replied, although I had no idea. I didn't even know it was a Northern Electric.

We plugged it in and, not knowing it took the tubes about thirty seconds to warm up, assumed it was not working until we heard some static. I fiddled with the dial until I came across the dulcet sounds of a saxophone.

"Very cool," said David.

"Yes," I said. "Very cool."

Three days later, my conscience got the better of me, and I tracked her down and returned the radio. I handed it to her and told her the coordinates for the jazz station, and she said, "ok, thanks."

And that was that.

Then, only 40 years later, I bought one of my own.

I had acquired this mini transmitter which allowed me to play music from my phone through a certain station on the radio.

First song I picked was *Staying Alive* by the Bee Gees.

But even though the radio sounded great, no hum at all, I couldn't make it past thirty seconds of listening. And then I put on Miles.

1949 CORONADO

I'm not sure who it is, but one of my neighbors likes to complain to the community association about my garden. This person has an issue with my weeds. So now I get constant reminders from the association to tend to my weeds. That is what they say – can I please tend to them. Turns out, that doesn't mean they want me to water them.

I have someone whom I pay to take care of my garden. I'm sure there is a way to say that which wouldn't make me sound like a dick. This person is not a very good gardener. Again, don't want to sound like a dick. He is a portly man who is originally from Haiti. He wears a big floppy hat. Now I'm sure a lot of people from Haiti are good gardeners. But Phillipe is just not one of them. That's his name. Phillipe 'Big Jean' Lecouche. I don't know how he gets Big Jean from Phillipe, but he insists I call him Big Jean. The thing is, I don't really care about my garden and would not even mention it if not for the complaints. When I told him about the weeds he said, "Mr. Ron, you know, I was not a gardener in Haiti. I was a doctor." Which, of course, is sad and heartbreaking and made me feel like shit. Until I found out he was actually a witch doctor. Which is still sad and heart breaking and made me feel like shit. But also - dick alert number three - a little bit funny.

Big Jean will sometimes come into the house for a drink and some air conditioning. He likes my radios. I have offered him the pick of the litter but he says, "Mr. Ron, I don't need a radio to hear the music."

I tell him, "Big Jean, that's beautiful. I'm going to use that in a story one day."

Big Jean hints that he has great powers he has yet to unleash. I don't know anything about voodoo, but he has picked the winner of eight basketball games in a row. Witch doctor indeed.

Now, 11:30pm to 12:30am is a bit of a witching hour for me. That's the time I search for radios online. And the time I put a lot of radios in my cart. In the morning, I remove 99% of them. That's also the time I put in bids for radios I probably don't want. In the early days of my collection addiction, I would get really upset when another collector, using what is called 'sniping software' would outbid me at the final second. Over time, that would change to me actually pumping my fist in the air and yelling out, "yes!" upon receiving an email from eBay informing me I had been outbid. It's like finding out your root canal has been cancelled.

One morning, I receive a box but am not really sure what radio it is. Both eBay and Etsy send notifications when items are delivered but I have received nothing. I have a few radios on the way but none that are marked as having been delivered. When I unbox the package, I pull out what I recognize as a Coronado. A Coronado I have absolutely no recollection of having bought. It is not on any of my purchased lists. I email my assistant, who sometimes facilitates the purchase of a radio, and ask if she had bought it. She says no.

The thing is. I don't like this radio. I have seen it many times and not bought it. I'm not a fan of this radio.

I email one of my dealers, Retro Radio Farm, and ask if they maybe shipped it by mistake. They say no. He sends me a copy of my email ordering it.

Even better, he has an email of me asking him to upgrade it to Bluetooth.

Ok then.

I look at the time stamp of my email. 1:15am. Now it makes sense.

Big Jean arrives late in the afternoon the next day. I have texted him and told him that we need to take care of the weeds. He has outfitted himself with all the implements of destruction. His truck, which is decorated in what can only be described as nouveau voodoo bumper stickers, is packed to the hilt. I help him unload a couple of jugs of liquid marked, in Road Runner fashion, with a big red X. Big Jean is either going to attack my weeds or is planning for an exorcism.

Possibly both.

It is a hot southern Florida day and he is already sweating profusely. I ask if he wants to come in for a drink. He beats me into the house.

He drinks his bottle of water in one big, noiseless gulp. Then, eyeing the Coronado, he says, "new radio Mr. Ron?"

The Coronado is no longer sitting alone on my kitchen table. Although I don't really like it, I have diligently put it on a shelf. I have hundreds of radios, and Big Jean picks it out right away.

"Yes," I say, "but I don't like it."

"You don't like it?"

"No."

"So why did you buy it?"

So, I tell him about the witching hour. He says, "Mr. Ron, are you making fun of me?" But he laughs when he says it. He looks at the radio and asks, "is it old?"

"1949," I reply.

"I am older," he says with another laugh. He runs his hand over the radio.

"Does it play?"

I plug it into my long extension cord and set it to Bluetooth. I tell Big Jean to pair it with his phone and then play a song.

"Anything?" he asks.

I say, "sure."

"I will play you a song from my home."

He then proceeds to play me an entire album. I don't mind. The music is hauntingly beautiful. I guess the words are in Creole. I don't speak Creole, but I understand every word. That's the thing about music.

Big Jean and I don't speak for an hour.

We just listen to the music.

I may have poured a glass or two of scotch.

It is dark outside when the last song ends.

I ask him if he wants the radio. He surprises me by saying yes. "I like this radio," he says. He looks outside.

"Too dark for weeds Mr. Ron," he says.

"Ok," I say.

The next day, I get up early to take out the recycling. Those guys come early. As I am dragging out the blue boxes, I look at my front lawn.

The weeds have all disappeared.

Vanished.

Just like that.

As I'm standing there, befuddled in my boxers, Maria from the association drives up.

"Mr. Zevy," she says, "it looks like my little reminders are working. I see that all the weeds are gone."

I nod my head. She hands me the notice she had planned to drop off in my mailbox.

Apparently, my roof now needs to be cleaned in order to meet the Association standards.

I'll have to get Big Jean another radio.

1950 HALLICRAFTERS CONTINENTAL

Goldfarb was in a funk.

Now Goldfarb was often in a funk and both Lewberg and I had learned to keep our heads down until it passed.

The problem this time was that Goldfarb had fallen into a funk right before the club team golf championship and we needed him for his drive. Goldfarb was not a great golfer, but he did hit his driver a long way, and we really needed that.

But now Goldfarb was in a funk.

The funk was not affecting his distance. He was still hitting a crazy long way. But he was not hitting it straight.

Not straight at all.

Lewberg decided it was my fault.

"You and your bloody radios," he said as Goldfarb hit another boomer into someone's house.

'You and your bloody radios' was a common refrain from Lewberg but today he was not entirely off the mark. I had received a new radio the day before. It was a 1950 Hallicrafters with a clock radio. It was very cheap and a little beat up. The eBay seller had advertised it as working, but that can sometimes mean no more than the radio turns on and makes a terrible hissing noise. Which was the case here. I didn't mind because I had two similar working models and had picked this one for no other reason than I liked the color.

Goldfarb was at the house when I unboxed it, tested it, then put it on the shelf. He didn't help me do any of those things but he was at the house. He won't say 'you and your bloody radios,' but he is often pained by what I spent and will sometimes say, "please tell me you didn't spend more than $50 for this piece of shit." Which was kinda what I was expecting but this time he said.

"We had that radio."

He said it in a very casual way. As if he was asking me to please pass the cream cheese.

A lot of people will come to the house and the radios will evoke memories. They will say, "we had that radio," or, "we had a radio just like that." Once or twice they will be curious enough to hunt down old family pictures and discover that the plastic Motorola radio they thought they had turned out to be wood. Memory plays tricks on you like that sometimes.

But Goldfarb was a scientist and if he said he had that radio, then he had that radio. I waited to see if he would say any more. Goldfarb is not the chatty type and, as Lewberg and I have learned, doesn't really like to talk about the old days that much.

For a second, I thought the moment had passed and then he said, "my father and I listened to Spassky-Fischer on that radio. BBC shortwave."

"Iceland 1972," I said.

"Yes," he replied.

This is where it pays to know a little bit about Goldfarb's history. Because otherwise, you might be left to think that a childhood memory of listening to chess with your father would evoke good memories.

But you would be wrong.

Goldfarb had been a chess prodigy who didn't want to be a chess prodigy. His father didn't care. Goldfarb had told me stories of how he listened to chess games on the radio, following along on his own chess board, and how his father then made him recreate the games by memory. Over and over again until he got it right.

Goldfarb, in defiance of his father, eventually quit chess but, not being able to give up gray matter pursuits entirely, took up backgammon.

It was a tough upbringing but I think he was more or less over it. In fact, both he and I had been playing the chess bots on chess.com lately. I asked him if he wanted to play me and he laughed so hard I thought he might pass out. But we both enjoyed watching YouTube videos from GothamChess, who was a 26-year-old named Levy Rozman, with 3.4 million subscribers, because he made his recaps of chess games, complete with exotic sounding names for openings and defenses, sound like a real sporting event.

So, I don't think it was the radio which put him into a funk. It was just a tiny trigger which put him in the funkdom lane for when the bigger trigger arrived.

And that trigger happened that very night.

Lewberg said we had to carbo load for the big match so the four of us went to an Italian joint we know. Golf is not exactly the tour de France but Lewberg took it pretty seriously so if he wanted to carbo load, who were we to question him?

Also, they made a delicious cacio e pepe.

We were into our third bottle of Barolo when two couples took the table next to us on the front patio. I didn't tell Lewberg that three bottles, which would soon become four, was not exactly the best preparation because Lewberg would have just said, "we're having

Italian. Do you want me to drink fucking San Pellegrino? Are we animals?" So, I didn't say anything but Lewberg and Solly, who was our fourth, were the only ones who could really hold their wine. In other words, when the other diners sat down, Goldfarb and I were pretty hammered.

Also, and this is on me, he was already a tiny bit triggered.

So, when the guy said what he said, which is something which over a million people have said in the last year, we should have suspected it might set Goldfarb off.

But I was too drunk.

Solly didn't care.

And Lewberg wasn't drunk enough.

What the guy said was, "oh my god, I loved the Queen's Gambit"

The Queen's Gambit, as many of you might know, was a very popular Netflix series about a chess player. It, combined with the pandemic, was partly responsible for the huge chess revival.

Upon hearing the name of the show, Goldfarb swiveled in his chair to face the speaker. We've seen this countless of times. This guy thought Goldfarb was about to say oh my god, I loved it too.

Now, Goldfarb has never said 'oh my god' in his life.

Also, he absolutely hated The Queen's Gambit even though the chess world universally said it was the most realistic depiction of chess ever on TV or film.

But Goldfarb didn't say he hated it. Instead, in a very calm tone which belied his volcanic mood, asked, "do you know what a Queen's Gambit is?"

The guy was a bit confused but not confused enough not to realize this was not going to go well. Still, he had enough composure to say "you know, the Netflix series."

Goldfarb, remaining seemingly calm, said, "yes, but the name of a series is based on a very famous, perhaps the most famous, chess opening. I'm just asking if you know what that opening is."

The guy shook his head no.

"Did you all watch the series?" he asked the others.

Goldfarb had so far not raised his voice. Had not used foul language. But even a fool could see that the blood and Barolo were boiling. He didn't wait for a response.

"Do any of you know what the queen's gambit is?"

They shook their heads.

"Nine episodes," Goldfarb calmly turned to me and said, "nine?"

And I said "I think so." I wasn't really sure what we were talking about.

"Nine episodes and nobody is curious to know what the queen's gambit opening is?"

The tirade that followed their collective head shaking was a thing of beauty. The waiter ushered us out about midway through. We heard the rest of it in the car. Goldfarb was partial to the phrase "Ignorant cretins." He used that one a lot.

"Ignorant cretins wouldn't know a knight fork if it got shoved up their asses."

"Ignorant cretins wouldn't recognize the Petrov Defense if Petrov himself was taking a shit in their bathroom."

That kind of thing.

Then Goldfarb got quiet.

When we got back to the house I got a laugh out of him by saying

"Ignorant cretins don't even understand you have to decline the gambit."

So, we thought maybe he was alright. Until he started hitting into the trees.

"Goldfarb is in a funk," Lewberg said as he sipped his Ketel and cran.

"Me and my bloody radios," I said with a smile beating him to it. We had finished fourth.

Behind the Garfinkel foursome. It was an embarrassment. Garfinkel was shit.

Lewberg said he didn't think he would be able to golf again for a week.

"Queen's gambit," he said.

"Ignorant cretins," I replied.

"We could take him to a basketball game," he said. "Knicks coming to town."

"Yeah, maybe," I replied. "Did you read that the Heat revoked Sovlar's 10-year naming deal for the stadium?"

"Yeah. Sorry Pappy." Lewberg was being kind. I had lost my shirt on a Sovlar crypto based NFT.

"Sovlar," I said. "Ignorant cretins."

"Naming rights," said Lewberg. "World has gone crazy."

"Yeah," I said. "Although," then I smiled, "it actually would be kinda funny. And Goldfarb would love it."

"What the hell are you talking about?"

"Naming rights."

"You want to name the Heat stadium after Goldfarb? Pappy, you're rich. But not that rich."

"Not the stadium."

"Then what?"

"A chess opening. I want to name a chess opening after Goldfarb."

And Lewberg. Good old Lewberg. He did not disappoint. Because then Lewberg said, "I think I've got a guy."

Now Lewberg did not have a guy. He had the guy. Zakarian.
Of the Zakarian Defense.

He was living, barely eking out an existence, this a former Armenian grandmaster, playing patzers for small change in Miami Beach. Twenty bucks to have your picture taken with the old Armenian. It was a travesty.

Lewberg and I offered him $10,000 for the naming rights. Lewberg was going to pay the whole thing himself with his NFT winnings. Unlike me, he got out early.

Zakarian agreed without batting an eyelash. He took the 10 grand, signed the papers, and then even charged me $20 for the picture we took.

The Zakarian Defense was now the Goldfarb Defense.

That part was easy.

Then we had to hire a lawyer to slap injunctions on the chess streamers who, by force of habit or stubbornness, refused to make the change.

I spoke to GothamChess himself and he assured me that he would adopt the new name.

The hardest part was fixing the Hallicrafters. It was a bitch to find the right part.

With my new transmitter, I could now transmit the YouTube video through the radio.

I invited Goldfarb over to listen. Lewberg came too.
The move comes very early in the game.

Rozman (aka GothamChess) described it very casually, "Not surprising to see Carlsen play the Goldfarb Defense here. That is what he often plays with the black pieces."

No reaction from Goldfarb.

So, I played it again.

Still no reaction.

Lewberg and I looked at each other. Lewberg shrugged his shoulder.

I said, "Goldfarb, anything you want to say?"

And Goldfarb said, "everyone knows he should have played the Petrov in this situation. The guy is a patzer."

Then he smiled.

Next day Goldfarb hit the ball long and straight.

1954 ZVEZDA RED STAR

Every once in a while, I will send Lewberg a text which says 'I have shelving issues.'

Lewberg will always reply with a 'Ha ha ha ha ha ha ha ha.'

Sometimes I will send it in response to a message he has sent complaining about one of the many things that ails him in his struggle to be Lewberg. And sometimes I will just send it out of the blue in order to get a laugh.

Lewberg and I are superstitious and we both understand that this is our way of warding off the evil eye.

I have bought a lot of radios and now have the problem of figuring out where to put them. This is not even a first world problem.

It is a 1% problem. Lewberg and I get it. It's my way of saying how lucky I am.

I didn't need a reminder. But if I did, the story of buying the 1954 Soviet Zvezda Red Star from Leon in Kyiv certainly drove it home for me.

To tell the story I have to begin with how and why I began collecting radios in the first place.

My friend Brian Green dropped by my house one day on his way home from work. After exchanging meaningless pleasantries, he said, "I bought a radio."

"Nice." At this point, which was pre-addiction and pre-obsession, I had no way of knowing if it was nice. But it seemed like the right thing to say.

"I have it in the car," he said.

Brian had a new radio and was excited to show it. I would soon understand that feeling. As would all of my friends and relatives. Since I am a good friend and maybe because I felt guilty that last year I showed no interest in seeing his new kitchen renovation, I said, "why don't you bring it in."

Brian went to his car and came back holding a 1950 Jewel Wakemaster. Here it is:

Right away I realized it was the exact same radio my parents had in their house when we were growing up!!

No. Not really. But that would have made sense. I had never seen this radio before.

But, for reasons neither I nor a team of eminent psychiatrists could have deduced, I thought it was very cool and I was immediately attracted to it. The design? The colors? The history? I have no idea.

I told Brian I thought it was cool and he was very pleased. "I knew you would like it" he said.

"You were right."

And then, in a moment that might offer a few more clues, I asked if I could hold it. I was just curious how heavy it was.

"Listen," I said, "would you be ok if I started collecting radios too?"

And Brian said, "it would be my honor."

Then I said "you understand I'm going to do it much better than you."

And he said "I have no doubt."

The first thing I had to do was research. So I went to the library. Jokes.

No, I went on Amazon, where I bought every book I could find on collecting radios - including one aptly titled The Idiot's Guide to Repairing Vintage Radios - and had them shipped to Florida where I was heading for the winter.

The book I was most excited about and the one which received the best feedback was Peter Sheridan's DecoRadio: the world's most beautiful radios. Sheridan was a dentist in Australia who had accumulated an unbelievable collection. The rumor was that an Emir from the Middle East had offered to buy the entire collection but Sheridan, fearing that the radios would be kept hidden away in a vault, turned him down.

The book had beautiful photos of radios from the years 1923 to 1956. My plan was to use it as a guide as to what I should start collecting.

Not that long ago, but it's hard to believe I was so naive and foolish.

I decided, thinking that the 'newer' radios would be easier to find, to start at the back. The last photograph was of the 1956 Oceanic Surcouf. Made in France, it was a stunning display of classic art deco design.

I Googled it.

Found it on, of all places, Etsy. I bought it. As a bonus, it came with Bluetooth.

You know how they say that the worst thing that can happen when you go to the casino for the first time is to win?

Well, using slot machine vernacular, I hit a 5-liner my first time out.

Ok, I didn't win any money. But I got the exact radio I had been looking for. I was on a roll.

Then, not.

The next radio, working backwards, was the 1954 Sparton Easy Goer in green. I couldn't find it. Still can't find it. While every seller on eBay describes their radios as rare and very hard to find, it turns out that there are many, many vintage radios that actually are really rare and virtually impossible to find.

That, as Bruce Springsteen says in Blinded by the Light, is 'where the fun is.' Are we having fun yet?

I decided to try another.

The 1954 Soviet made Zvezda Red Star. Here is the page, printed without permission, from Sheridan's book:

Made by the Russian military as a showcase of their design ability. If the names of European towns and cities on the Surcouf was cool, then those on the Zvezda, all in Cyrillic, were super cool.

I Googled it.

And there, right on eBay, was a listing. A Zvezda in mint condition. Being shipped from, I squinted to read the small print on my phone, from the Ukraine. Wow! This was the real deal. I scrolled through the pictures. What a beauty! I could make a bid or, in a feature I would frequently take advantage of, pay a little more and Buy Now.

I wasn't going to risk losing this baby! I bought now. And then I waited.

I checked eBay. Radio was paid for but showing as still not shipped. And then the Russians invaded the Ukraine.

Lewberg texted me, 'The Russians are screwing up your radio collection.' Lewberg was kidding.

But, it turned out, he was, sadly, right on the money. The Russians were screwing up my radio collection.

I know because I received a message from Leon, the eBay seller and current holder of the Zvezda.

He was, in a note he wrote in perfect English and one which broke my heart 'very, very sorry.' Could I please accept his apologies? The Russians had bombed his apartment complex. He was now, along with his wife and three kids, living with his mother in law in an undisclosed location. He had the radio with him. It was all packed up and ready to go. He was just waiting until the post office resumed service so he could ship it. Could I please, he urged, just wait a little more?

I wrote him back and said to forget about the radio. Just stay safe. Don't worry about it. All good. I would give him a 5-star review and not say anything to eBay. He could keep the money and the radio. Please, please. Just stay safe.

Leon wrote back immediately and said he was in a very safe place. That he appreciated my concern. But it was no problem. It was just an issue with the post office. I wrote back to say it was ok. I didn't need the radio. Two days later he wrote to say it was on the way. He didn't say it but I had a feeling that he wasn't going to let the Russians screw up my collection.

Then I waited.

Then I waited some more.

When the radio finally arrived, I knew right away something was wrong. The box was mangled and torn. When I carried it in from the front door I could hear parts jingling.

I feared the worst. I opened the box.

The radio, or what was left of it, has been completely destroyed. I shuffled the broken parts around for a few minutes to see if anything could be salvaged, but it was a complete write-off.

Such a shame.

I dragged the box to the curb. Garbage day was tomorrow.

Then I logged onto eBay, gave Leon 5 stars in every category, and left a very nice review. And that, was that.

Or, so I thought.

A week later I heard from Leon. He thanked me for my review.

I should not feel obligated but would I be interested in a 1952 Tesla Radio from Czechoslovakia?

I looked in the book.

The Tesla was on page 149.

'Sure,' I said. 'Why not?'

'Great,' he replied. 'I will ship. But I have to tell you it is not in as good shape as the Zvezda.'

I said, 'no problem.'

1954 SPARTON FOOTBALL

I have a lot of radios.

When visitors come to my house in Florida, they can't help but be overwhelmed by the display of radios. The most common comment is - well, the most common comment is, "you really need to find yourself a woman," - but after that, it is, "do they all work?"

It is a bit of a tricky question because, although the great majority do work, they don't get very good, or actually any, reception where I live. So, I end up giving Bill Clinton-like answers – 'it depends on your definition of works'.

I would turn the radio on, wait 30 seconds for the tubes to heat up, then turn the dial around and get various degrees of static. On occasion, you could detect a hint of voices and a soupçon of what might have been Caribbean music. My friend Allie, the kind soul that she is, said she thought she could hear a few notes of Steely Dan. But mostly just static. After a while, when asked if they worked, I would just say no and leave it at that. Until my ex-girlfriend came to town.

Now, this ex-girlfriend, like all of my ex-girlfriends, was happily married. Everything and everyone begins to look great after a few months with me. I actually quite liked her husband and thought nothing of suggesting they drop by if they found themselves in my 'hood. I guess you could say I'm doing better now than I was when we were together, but I'm not sure how far away being alone with a house full of radios is from being alone with a house full of cats, and I'm not really sure anyone is keeping score. Although, I think she was.

So, when she said, "oh, what a beautiful pool," it was hard for me not to hear that she was really saying was, 'I hope you drown in it.'

This is only to say that she derived a great amount of joy upon discovering that the radios did not actually work.

For about 45 minutes, I think 'static' was her all-time favorite word. Not only that, she was visually ecstatic every time she heard static coming out of a radio. At one point, she gleefully said, "listen, static in stereo."

I don't know what it is about ex-girlfriends.

I have no regrets.

I have no second thoughts.

But, be that as it may, the very next day, I decided to make the damn radios work.

I began with antennas. My house was soon filled with coiled wires and antennas of every shape and form. Still static. The first glimmer of hope came when one of my radio dealers, one who ironically really only cared about the mint appearance of the radios, told me there was a vintage radio store, in Alberta, Canada no less, which advertised a homemade mini radio transmitter. This was a metal box, about a third of the size of a tissue box, which you could connect to your iPhone. If you placed the transmitter directly behind a radio, it would then transmit the music to a megahertz band, in this case, it was 1150, on your AM tube radio. Unlike with Bluetooth, you would actually have to tune into a station, literally your own radio station - with a range of only three feet - and the music would play through the radio as it did seventy years ago. Best of all, it was only $79.

"Do you think it will work?" I asked.

"Doesn't hurt to try," she said.

So, I ordered one, peppered the owner with tons of questions, and waited patiently for my transmitter to arrive.

When it did, I was like a kid on Christmas morning. Not a Jewish kid. But you get what I mean.

I called Fernando, my handyman, and his assistant José. Now, the woman I bought the transmitter from told me that setting it up would be child's play. But she had no idea who she was dealing with. I'm not as smart as a child. And twice as lazy. This thing had wires and a metal enclosure which required the use of a screwdriver. I did not own a screwdriver. José and Fernando tried for four hours, including a one-hour conversation with the woman in Alberta, but could not elicit a single peep from any of the five radios we tried. It turned out, they all agreed, that there was just too much interference in the area for it to work. Which is why we couldn't tune in to any regular station. She was going to send a replacement transmitter just in case the first got damaged in delivery, but none of us were holding our breath. All of these radios. And not a single song. I was crestfallen.

Listen, I'm not an idiot. First world problems and all. But still, it really sucked. José felt so bad that he gifted me his screwdriver. At 3 am, I got up to pee. Also, at 1 am, and 2 am. But, that's not part of the story. I walked to the dining room, where we had left the transmitter, and turned on the light. The transmitter had come with instructions, and now I read them for the first time. Remove the back and insert a 9-volt battery. I used José's screwdriver and unscrewed the four screws and removed the back. It already had a battery. I flicked the On/Off button a few times but no dice. Then, I removed the battery and put it back in, making sure it was tight and secure. Still no dice. Then, because I'm nothing if not a quitter, I put the back cover back on, deftly screwed in the four screws, and went back to bed.

At 4 am, I got up to pee.

Which, as you may have figured out, was not unusual. But, I also had an idea. Which was very unusual.

I went to my radio display. I grabbed a working transistor radio. I then removed the back from that transistor, unclasped the 9-volt battery, went to the dining room, turned on the light, unscrewed the four screws with José's screwdriver, removed the back, replaced the battery in the transmitter with the one I had removed from the transistor, and then tried the On/Off switch.

And a light came on.

And god said that was good.

I then grabbed the same Sparton which Allie said she could maybe hear Steely Dan from, plugged it in, waited thirty seconds, tuned the dial to 1150, attached the transmitter to my iPhone, placed the transmitter directly behind the Sparton, found the song I wanted on YouTube, and then hit play. And music came from the speakers of the 1954 Sparton Football. It wasn't crisp. It wasn't clear. It crackled a little. But it was music. Coming from the radio.

And god said it was good.

I then played the song again and, using a second phone mind you, took a twenty-second video of the radio playing. I then texted the video to Fernando and José and Allie. I was so excited I didn't know if I would fall asleep. I had half a mind to stay up and make videos of music playing on my radios all night. But I went to bed and I fell asleep. In the morning, Allie sent me a text.

'What am I looking at?'

'My radio playing music.'

'Through the transmitter?'

'Yup.'

'Nice. Are you going to send it to,' and then she mentioned the name of my ex-girlfriend.

And I said, 'of course not. This has nothing to do with her.'

And Allie said, 'Of course not.'

But, it just so happened that the aforementioned ex-girlfriend was in town for a convention, and I prevailed on her to come over to check out the radios in action. And so, she did. And I did my little transmitter song and dance. And by some strange coincidence, I may have picked out songs that some people may have remembered as 'our songs.' I mean, I don't really remember. After I was all done with the presentation, she said, "let me get this straight. Every time you want to play a radio, you gotta drag this little box around, and it won't play unless it's sitting right behind the radio?"

So, what could I say? I had to say, "yes."

Then she said, "okay."

But it was the way she said it.

If you now think the very first thing I did the minute she walked out of the house was to order a $2,200 transmitter from a company in Norway, which promised it could get reception for any and every radio I owned from any and every room in my house, well, you would have been 100% right. That is exactly what I did. I had to wait six months. Not for the transmitter. The transmitter came right away, but it was six months before the ex-girlfriend came back. But I waited. This time she brought her sister. It was, as best as I could tell, a shared schadenfreude. The exhibition could not have gone better. Jazz and blues from every room in the house, plus from a transistor all the way on the actual 17th green. The Norwegian transmitter worked like a charm. Not even a hint of static. It was a coup de force.

"Wow," said my ex-girlfriend, "it's like you have your own radio station."

Now she got it; she really got it.

"So, what do you think?" I asked.

And I didn't see it coming.

Because she smiled and then said, "I think you really need to get yourself a woman."

1955 FIRESTONE

I had never been on eBay before I started collecting radios. To be honest, it all seemed, I wasn't sure why, a little nefarious. Even when I began bidding for and buying radios on the site, I didn't have my own account. I didn't want to get involved. Didn't want to enter a credit card. I wanted to keep an arm's length distance. I asked one of my employees to buy the radios for me and he would then expense them. But he lives in the UK and the time difference sometimes made it hard to get messages about what I wanted out in time. Also, we lost a couple of bids on radios I wanted, so I decided I would take over the reins.

Collecting and addiction are separate words, but I'm not entirely sure they are all that different. I used to mock all of the people who logged unfathomable hours checking their Instagram and TikTok, until I began to visit eBay multiple times a day. And night.

Multiple. Because eBay has replaced garage and estate sales as the place to rummage through vintage wares in the hope of finding that rare and hard to find (HTF in eBay lingo) radio. Hoping that some poor shmuck who usually sold Grateful Dead signed programs had inherited his grandfather's rare Addison catalin and listed it for $49 - but was open to offers. It never happened. But it didn't stop us from refreshing the site and checking for new listings.

I got to know the vernacular and the type of personalities. From the sellers who were so careful not to mislead and disappoint that they would say 'it was playing this morning but please consider it as a bonus if it works', to those who applied every marketing trick of the trade. Everything was rare. Everything was hard to find. Everything played as if new. And, of course, the greatest pitch of all - 'just discovered in the attic.' Despite all that, when I came across this iconic Firestone with the imitation Mercedes Tri-Star, which was advertised as an 'attic find' with a touching 'graduation gift from Mom and Dad. Colleen 1955' written on masking tape fixed on the back, I snapped it right up with a high bid. The radio didn't work and was only in ok shape, but I loved those Tri-Star radios, and the masking tape, that piece of history, made it a no-brainer. Oh, the stories that radio could tell (now my nieces are all saying - Uncle Ronnie, you're the writer. You should tell the story about Colleen and not waste our time telling us about how you bought it on eBay. But I don't know Colleen. And anyways, I only write the truth).

I have to say I was pretty damn pleased with my buy. It was, in large part, why I got into collecting in the first place.

I showed the radio and the masking tape message to everyone who walked into the house.

It was a great story.

Until Lewberg came over.

Lewberg scoffed when I showed him the radio.

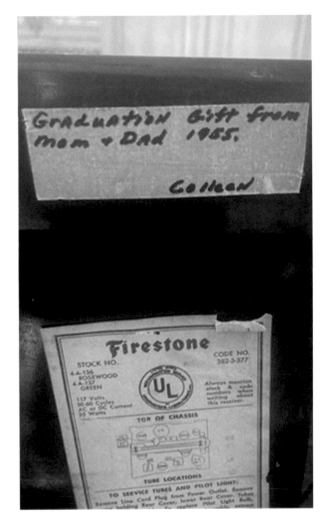

"You fell for the oldest trick in the book," he said shaking his head. "The old graduation gift on the masking tape." He said it like Maxwell Smart.

"Just classic," he continued, "the guy saw you coming from a mile away."

I wasn't sure why Lewberg was talking like he was in a 1955 movie, but he was pissing me off.

"Lewberg," I countered, "you have no clue. The radio wasn't even that expensive. I'm sure the masking tape is genuine."

"It works?" he asked.

"No."

"A little scuffed up," he continued, running his fingers along the case.

"Yeah," I admitted.

"You asked your collector friend?" he asked.

"Yeah."

"What did she say?"

I didn't like the way this was going. "She said I overpaid," I said sheepishly.

"Well, there you go," he said waving his arms, "case closed. Now enough with the radios. Can you pour me a Ketel and cran?"

But I wasn't ready to let it go.

"You really think that someone is going to go to the trouble of faking a masking tape note for the sake of a couple hundred bucks?"

"Well..."

"You bought it on eBay?"

"Yeah."

"Well," he said, helping himself to my vodka, "I'm sure it is full of honest people. Keep looking. Maybe you will find a transistor radio previously owned by Benjamin Franklin."

Of course, I didn't care what Lewberg thought. And even if he was right, what difference did it make? It was a perfectly nice radio regardless of whether it had a nice story attached to it.

I took out my iPad and logged into my eBay account.

I searched through my purchases to find the Firestone. I clicked on it.

The seller's account had been suspended. "Damn," I said out loud. "Damn, damn."

"What are you looking at there, Pappy?" he asked with a wide grin.

"ESPN," I replied sullenly. "I lost my football bet." Then I looked at the radio and the masking tape again.

I shook my head.

I wasn't going to let it bother me.

There is no direct flight from Miami to St. Paul, MN. You have to go through Chicago. I'm sure the good folks of Minneapolis/St. Paul would disagree, but there really is no good reason to leave Florida in the dead of winter and go to Minnesota.

But that is where the 3M headquarters were located. And 3M manufactured masking tape.

The guy I was going to see was called James Wilkenson. It only took me 18 emails and 22 phone calls.

After a while, I finally realized that opening with, "I'm looking for someone who can carbon date masking tape," was not a productive approach. To be honest, I was kinda surprised that they didn't have an entire department for this sort of thing. In the end, I got through to someone at the 3M Historical Society and that person said, "the person you want to see is Jim Wilkenson."

Now I think it is ridiculous and offensive that any person from the lovely state of Minnesota is automatically and callously relegated to having an accent like a character from Fargo, but you can call Jim Wilkenson and decide for yourself.

That's all I'm going to say.

I didn't really want to disparage him because he was the first person to take me semi-seriously.

Well, until I told him I wasn't going to send him the masking tape. "You're not going to send me the tape?" he asked.

"No," I replied, "I'm afraid I'm going to rip it."

"The masking tape?"

"Yeah. I really don't want to rip it."

"I see." Jim Wilkenson was super patient. "So how am I going to test it?"

"I thought I would bring the radio to you."

"'I see," he said. "Why don't you just ship it?"

"I'd rather not," I said. "I don't really trust those shippers. I've lost a few radios that way. And have had a few damaged."

"I see," said Jim Wilkenson, "so this is a rare and expensive radio?"

"No," I replied, "it is pretty common. Not rare at all."

"I see," he said, although it was becoming clear that he did not see at all. "This Colleen, she was famous? Or became famous?"

"I don't think so. I'm not sure she is even real."

Then Jim Wilkenson said, "well, better bundle up, we're having one of those winters."

I said, "ok."

Then I thought he said, "global warming my ass."

It took Jim Wilkenson all of thirty-seven seconds to tell me it was real. Maybe thirty-eight.

"That's it?" I said.

"You were expecting some fancy X-ray machine?" he said.

"What gave it away?" I asked.

"I could tell you but I would have to kill you."

Nah. He didn't say that. He said, "it's old masking tape. What can I tell you?"

Jim Wilkenson gave me a drink of scotch from a bottle he had in his desk. Made some joke about scotch and scotch tape which he had likely made a hundred times before.

We drank our scotch and then he asked, "does she work?"

I shrugged my shoulders. "Nope. Just humming."

"Really? Let's open her up. Might be a loose tube."

He then pulled out a screwdriver from the same desk drawer he had found the scotch in and effortlessly removed the back panel.

"Ya see? That number 4 tube is loose. That often happens with these old babies." He then wriggled around and pushed the tube so the prongs easily entered their respective holes.

Then he plugged it in.

Thirty seconds later, we heard the same hum I had heard in Florida. And then he turned the knob until he got to 1280.

It came in loud and clear.

AM 1280 in Minneapolis/St. Paul. The Patriot.

You can look it up.

Loud and clear. Disc jockey was predicting more snow. "You see," said Jim, "just a loose tube."

When I got back Lewberg asked where I had been. He hadn't seen me on the course for a few days.

"I went to a radio shop and got the Firestone fixed. Plays nice now."

Of course, I couldn't tell Lewberg that the masking tape was real. That it was really from 1955. Couldn't tell him or anyone that I flew to St. Paul with a stop in Chicago with the Firestone radio securely wrapped in my overnight bag in order to see Jim Wilkenson.

Couldn't tell him that security both in Miami and St. Paul twice made me unwrap and then rewrap the radio because they wanted to see what was in the bag. Or about the Uber getting stuck in the snow, or about having to wait 45 minutes for another Uber in the freezing cold because apparently nobody wants to be an Uber driver in Minnesota in the winter.

I got him a Ketel and cran, cranked up the transmitter and put on some Ella.

"Not bad," said Lewberg. "Sounds pretty good. How much did he charge you to fix it?"

"Not a dime. Did it for free," I answered truthfully. "Plus, he gave me a drink of scotch."

"There you go Pappy. Maybe you're not such a sucker after all."

I would have given him the thumbs up, but it had gotten frostbite waiting for the second Uber on the side of the road.

Instead I turned up Ella and thought about Colleen and the stories that radio would be able to tell.

1956 ZENITH ROYAL

Having never been married, I don't think it is a stretch to say I have an aversion to relationships. On the other hand, I didn't mind the odd entanglement. The woman who I now wanted to be entangled with had recently been divorced. I had pursued this woman spectacularly unsuccessfully before she got married and now providence, conveniently disguised as a cheating husband, was giving me another kick at the proverbial can.

I often complain to Allie that things never seem to fall into my lap - and when they do, they are invariably accompanied by a kick in the groin - but in this instance I had to admit that things were looking sunny in Floradelphia.

To begin with, she reached out to me. Now it was not the first time a woman had made the first move, but the two previous times they had been calling from American Express and Visa respectively. Plus, she was coming to me. She was going to spend the winter in Boca. In a community not five minutes from my own. And to top it off, not only did she not know anyone in Florida other than her aged aunts, but she had sworn off dating apps and any sort of fix ups.

As my late father used to say, in the land of the blind, the one-eyed man is king. And I, after a long, long wait, was finally the man with only one eye.

Lewberg, who had been around during my first falls and fails, said he was very excited.

"I know you are going to screw it up," he said, "the fun is going to be watching just how."

So, this woman and I started dating. I say dating, but I may be taking poetic license with the word because although what we were doing had all the appearances of dating, it really wasn't dating at all. Put another way, ever so delicately, I may have been the king of the land, but I was definitely not collecting any taxes.

Now the problems and issues she may have had with me in this department are no doubt too long to list or to mention, but since the theme of all these stories are radios, let us, for the sake of argument, say that her number one issue was my radios.

While there are radios in nearly every room in my house, the room where they are the most prominent is my bedroom. On the far wall, I have constructed a floor to ceiling shelf all filled with radios. It is one of my favorite places in the world.

This woman said the room made her uncomfortable. It was a constant reminder she was dating a man who was a little bit off. Needless to say, I would have been quite open to any other room. My mind once even wandered to the prospect of the golf cart in the garage. But no, she said, if this was going to work out, she would have to come to terms with the fact I collected radios. It's not so much that she didn't like the radios. It's just that she didn't like the fact that anyone could or would ever want to do such a thing. It wasn't that she was bemused - she was downright embarrassed. In the meantime, the coffers of the kingdom were bare. I didn't mind striking out a second time - god knows I was no stranger to the swing and the miss - but why lay the blame of the 'no lay' on these poor radios? I was ready to throw in the towel and the tubes when came a glimmer of hope. It came, as luck would have it, in the form of a radio. You know how a flu vaccine is sometimes made with part of the same flu? Well I was about to inoculate her with a dose of Zenith.

I had bought this Zenith Royal Transistor on eBay and the seller was telling me what a great deal I got even though I had just paid him what he was asking and hadn't bargained at all. He was a very nice person and emailed me every day to give me the status of the box. But he kept going over and over about what a great deal I got and I kinda sensed he was having seller's remorse. I get how you can get attached to an item like that. So, I offered to ship it back. No hard feelings. But he said no, no, he just was letting me know what a great deal I was getting because both the radio and leather case were in mint shape. So, then I wrote back how ironic it was because I didn't even keep the cases. And he said, 'what do you mean?' And I said, 'well, I only collect the radios, not the cases.'

The case, he said, was mint. I gently told him I didn't collect cases.

I kinda thought he would just cancel the order and ask me to ship it back but instead, he asked that, if I wasn't keeping it, would I mind shipping the case back.

He was pretty nice about it so, even though it was a pretty weird request, it was really no skin off my, is it nose, so I agreed.

This woman I was not really dating had not said anything as crazy as 'it's either the radios or me,' but it seems I had given her the impression that I was done with radios and in fact had started to, as we collectors say, thin out my collection. Now I'm not sure where she got that impression but I have heard of many a monarch who literally lost their minds because they were not collecting taxes. I'm just saying.

And so, king or not, one eye or not, I began to treat the arrival of packages containing radios, packages whose frequency if anything increased, as a bit of a covert operation. Luckily, my sharing of my golf cart pseudo fantasy proved to be a blessing in disguise because she now avoided the garage like the bubonic plague. I was disposing of cardboard boxes, much like Tim Robbins in Shawshank, in different recycling bins on the street. The new radios I tucked away on shelves behind the paint cans.

Every once in a while, I would remove a radio from the shelf in my bedroom and announce, "just sold another one," then stow it away in the garage. It might have been my imagination, but I felt the hugs and kisses, such as they were, were increasing in intensity. It was only a matter of time until, I'm just going to go ahead and say it, no more euphemisms, that we were going to have sex in the radio room.

And then she caught me.

It was the Zenith transistor. I had brought it into the house only to see, for a moment, how it would look on the shelf. Also, I was looking for some tape so I could send back the case.

That's when she caught me red-handed.

There was a moment of silence and I prepared for the worse. Then she said, "is that leather?" Then she said, "oh my god, that case is sooo cute!"

Then she said, "why did you never tell me about those cases?"

If I had been paying attention, I might have noticed that transistor radio leather case "sooo cute," was not the same as Louis Vuitton leather purse "soooooooooo cute."

But I wasn't paying attention.

So, I didn't ship back the case. The seller gave me a one-star review, complete with a very long harangue about how badly I treated cases and how nobody should deal with me.

Which would have been all fine and worth it if she hadn't started dating a Miami Heat player a few days later.

Turns out, it wasn't the radios after all.

I got my second eye back, and although I still had no taxes, I had a really nice view of my radios.

1956 HALLICRAFTERS IN DIJON YELLOW

I was having lunch at the club with a woman I was seeing at the time. In addition to being very beautiful, she was also a tiny bit younger than me. Also, on that particular day, she had come directly to lunch from the Pilates class she had been teaching. So, she was still in her Lululemon attire.

We were having lunch on the terrace overlooking the 18th green and were seated at a table next to three tennis ladies. I didn't know them, though that wasn't unusual because I don't really know anyone, but I gave them a friendly wave because it is a friendly club and I pretty much wave at everyone.

One of the ladies, in a flamingo pink tennis dress, said, "I don't know you. Are you a new member?"

This kind of stuff doesn't really bother me, and also, maybe a bigger factor, I'm on really good meds, so I replied, "fairly new, I've only been here 7 years."

Then I smiled.

"That's odd," she said, "I'm such a social butterfly, I thought I knew everyone. What street do you live on?"

Even in such a small community as ours, the street you live on bestows some sort of social status.

"Valencia," I said, pointing in the vague direction of my street.

Then I said what I always say in these situations. "I moved into Larry Sharnak's old house. I golf with him."

Larry used to be a board member, and, for reasons I find unfathomable, is generally beloved in our community. Basically, I was going for acceptance by association.

Then all 3 nodded their heads. Of course, they knew Larry.

I could now order my half chicken salad sandwich with a side of coleslaw.

But first, the flamingo pink dress needed to take a shot.

"It's so nice you can have lunch with your daughter. My kids live so far away in California."

I'm not sure what I would have said. Luckily, one of her lunch mates, in a Dijon yellow dress, wisely decided to save the day.

"I'm Deborah Mason," she said. Then introductions were made all around.

"Are you retired Ron?" asked Deborah.

"No," I answered.

"What do you do?"

So, this is when I lied. I guess I was still a bit irritated over the 'lunch with your daughter' comment.

Now, although I lie all the time, I really don't ever lie about my job. The only time was when my friend Bernie and I went to Club Med and I told people I played the triangle for the Toronto Symphony.

"I'm an artist," I said.

"Painter?"

One of our members, Larry Dinkin, was a very well-respected painter with pieces in over forty museums.

"No, no. I'm a conceptual artist."

"How interesting," said Flamingo Pink in a tone which implied it wasn't interesting at all.

"Yes, I make arrangements of vintage radios and then photograph them. A little in the style of Dale Chihuly."

It wasn't in the style of anyone. I owned a 1000-piece Chihuly puzzle of an installation of radios he had in Seattle. I just put radios on my shelves and took pictures. I had a few on my phone. To be honest, they could be art.

Then Deborah, pointing to the third woman, who had yet to speak, said, "you know Linda has a gallery in Palm Beach."

Just my luck.

"Is your work being shown anywhere?" asked Linda. She said it while eyeing my date's Lululemon outfit. Also, in a judgmental tone which made Flamingo Pink seem kind and understanding.

Now of course, I could have just said, "just kidding," and retreated as gracefully as I could have.

But then I'd be left with a half-finished story. Instead, I decided to dig myself a little deeper.

"God no," I said as haughtily as I could muster, "I didn't think anyone did physical art anymore. All my stuff is NFTs. Gotta be on the blockchain. Crypto is the future."

I didn't believe that at all.

So now they would ask what NFTs were, and I would say, "non-fungible tokens," hoping I pronounced fungible properly.

Then one of them would say, "never heard of them."

Then my date, who was not a stranger to my fabrications, would pipe up with a zinger.

"That's probably because," she would then take a long sip of her unsweetened tea, "you're too damn old."

Ok. So, a little short but that would have been a perfectly good ending. Nice funny story. Move on.

But no.

Because, after I said NFT, Deborah, Dijon Yellow, said, "oh, like Bored Apes."

Then Flamingo Pink said, "Ethereum is the best."

And then Linda said, "I have two NFT installations at my gallery. Can you send me a link?"

The chicken sandwich was as good as ever but it felt like I was choking on it.

My date was not thrilled that I said no to the waiter's offer for cappuccino, and I sped my golf cart back to the house. When I got home, I called Lewberg and explained my situation.

As always, Lewberg said, "I've got a guy." Lewberg's guy wanted $1200 for the mining costs.

I didn't know very much about this but I'd done some research on Ethereum, and that seemed like a lot.

Lewberg said, "it's not Ethereum. It is Sovlar."

I told Lewberg I didn't know what that was. He said not to worry. "It is a new cryptocurrency token that is linked to the American dollar."

I didn't know what that meant, but I wired him the money.

I now had five NFTs of photographs of radios on a shelf. I titled them RadiosOnShelf1, RadiosOnShelf2, RadiosOnShelf3, RadiosOnShelf4, and RadiosOnShelf5. Here's what they looked like:

RadioOnShelf1

RadioOnShelf2

RadioOnShelf3

RadioOnShelf4

RadioOnShelf5

To make them look like digital art, we ran them through a program. The whole thing was ridiculous.

Lewberg's guy asked how much I wanted to sell them for. I said $1000 each. I figured the tennis ladies could afford it. I wasn't wrong. I sent the link and they each bought one. As I suspected, the woman in the Dijon yellow dress bought the Dijon yellow Hallicrafters. Then Lewberg bought one.

I said, "Lewberg, the whole thing is a scam. This is just me covering up a lie."

Lewberg said, "Pappy, I believe in you."

Linda put her Zevy NFT, RadiosOnShelf4, on display in her gallery. Within 2 weeks, it sold for $18,000. The others sold for more. Lewberg got an offer from an overseas buyer for $42,000.

"Pappy you're a genius," he exclaimed.

I decided to wait until it hit $100,000. Not because of the money.

But because I thought 'The $100,000 NFT' was a great title for the story.

Also, I might have gotten a bit greedy.

So maybe it was a little bit about the money. Also, I had started to plan #6, 7, 8, and 9.

Now, I don't want to throw my now ex-girlfriend under the bus. But it was her idea that we spend two days in the Bahamas without our cell phones.

She said it would be romantic.

She said it was only two days.

What could possibly happen in two days?

Of course, you by now have all read about Andrew Sovlar and what happened to his eponymous crypto currency. He was arrested at his Bahamas mansion not three miles from where I was enjoying my cell-free weekend.

RadiosOnShelf1, the one I kept for myself, was now worth $4. "Lewberg," I said, "you screwed me."

And Lewberg said, "Pappy, the pain is what makes you a great artist."

1956 MOTOROLA 56CC2

My family likes to watch movies down in the basement after dinner when we are at the cottage. Although I like movies as much as the next guy, maybe even more, I don't really like to watch movies with the family. In large part because they start way too late, take way too long to choose, end up choosing a movie I don't want to see, and also - and I can't stress this point too much - it's way too cold down there. Anyway, to their credit, they always try to get me to watch a movie with them. And I always say no.

I had already gone to my room in the bunkie when Caroline, my sister in law, texted me to say, 'Ron, we are going to watch the Elvis movie.'

Now I generally hate biopics and have really little or no interest in Elvis or his manager Colonel Parker. But I put on two sweatshirts and my warmest socks and hurried back to the basement.

I had been dying to see that movie. For one reason, and one reason only. My radio was in it.

Early that year, I had purchased a 1955 Zenith from eBay. The seller, ostensibly a prop shop, claimed that it had been used in the new Elvis movie which was shot in Australia.

A few weeks after I received the radio, I got a message from the seller saying it appeared for a few seconds at the thirty-minute mark.

Which I thought was very cool.

Apparently, I had spent a good amount of time over that summer telling people my radio was in the Elvis movie. If my friends and family are to be believed, there was no question I could be posed to which I didn't answer, "my radio is going to be in the Elvis movie."

Anyway, there was indeed a brief close-up at the 30-minute mark, and my nieces may have said something to the effect of, "wow, that's cool Uncle Ron," and that was about it. The radio didn't work. It was just a prop in a movie. Now it was on my shelf.

A couple of weeks later, I was going through the listings on eBay when I came across a 1956 Motorola 56CC2 in pink. I actually already owned that radio so I didn't bid on it or spend too much time looking at the listing. I was about to move on when I noted the seller was advertising it as the Goodfellas radio. Goodfellas is an iconic movie about the mafia and it is a favorite of many - including myself. I Googled it, trying different combinations of words and descriptions but came up empty. So, I messaged the seller and asked. He or she wrote back very quickly with but one line: 'Go to YouTube and search Goodfellas shower scene.'

So, I did.

And this is what I found:

https://www.youtube.com/watch?v=pqE66RltUaQ

Now, to be clear, I didn't have the radio which was in the movie. I just had the exact same kind and color of radio which was in the movie.

Nonetheless.

Everybody thought this was super cool. From then on, a tour of my radios included a showing, and sometimes reshowing of the YouTube clip, then an in-person viewing of the radio.

"Wow. That is very cool! That is the exact same radio," is what people would say.

I would do an 'aw shucks' and reply, "now, now, that's not the actual radio that was in the movie. Just the exact same kind of radio."

And people would wave me off and say, "no c'mon, that's so cool."

I would then say, "let me show you this very rare Emerson Catalin in mint condition," and the person would say, "can I see that clip again?"

So, that went on for a while.

One night, Goodfellas was showing on TV. I had seen it many times but not in a while so I decided to watch it again. By the time the shower scene came around, I had already figured it out. The only solace I could take was that nobody else, not even my sometimes- cynical lawyer friend Steve, had also figured it out. I pressed pause and went online. I already knew what I would find. Goodfellas takes place in the 50s, when Henry Hill, played by the late Ray Liotta, is a teenager, and goes all the way to the late 70s. Hill is in the shower and cries out, "Jimmy," upon learning, by way of the news broadcast on the pink 1956 Motorola, that there has been a heist at the Lufthansa terminal.

Which occurred in 1978.

1956 radio in 1978. Could happen.

But I didn't think so.

Now I don't want to be that guy. But seriously. That aint right.

What was Scorsese thinking?

So, when my cousin Jeff and his son Oliver came over about a week later to say hello and so that Oliver could see my transistor radios, I showed Jeff the clip, and he said, "you know that's my favorite movie."

And I said, "take the radio."

And he said, "no I couldn't."

Then I said, "you'd be doing me a personal favor," (like the pen which writes upside down).

So, he took the radio and I was happy to be rid of it because it only reminded me of how the prop guy had screwed up one of my favorite movies.

And that would have been the end of it if my neighbor, Gladys Horn, had not decided to rent out her house.

Gladys Horn was a very nice lady in her mid-fifties who inherited a brick bungalow from her parents. She and I had the only two remaining original 1950s bungalows left on the street. All the others had been torn down and replaced with behemoths. Both Gladys and I were constantly accosted by real estate agents wanting to buy our houses. I turned them down. Me, because I was too lazy, and Gladys, well Gladys, and I hate to say it, because she was too greedy.

Sorry Gladys.

So, when the guy from the production house knocked on my door asking if I wanted to rent out my house for a week or two for a movie shoot set in the 50s - and then he told me how much they were paying - I sent him to Gladys down the street. I don't like strangers in my house. I don't even like people I know in my house. When my family will be coming over for dinner, I encourage them to go to the bathroom at their house first.

Well Gladys Horn might have been greedy but she was not graceless. The next day she arrived with a box of chocolates to thank me for my reference. Then she told me how much she was getting.

It was more than what they had offered me. Good old Gladys.

Then Gladys told me who was going to be in the movie. It was the name of an actress you would know.

Not hugely famous. But pretty famous. I was actually a fan.

Not enough to let her use my bathroom. But a fan.

Gladys told me a little about what the movie was about, although she was sworn to secrecy, and it sounded all very nice and she had negotiated allowing three of her friends to watch the shoot, and I could come too because I had been so nice. But I had been on a movie shoot before and it was actually deathly boring, so I deferred.

As she was leaving, I said to her, "do you know the prop guy?"

And she said she did not know the prop guy.

She didn't even know what a prop guy was. So, I explained it to her and she asked me what I wanted the prop guy for, and I said that since it was set in the 1950s they might want an age-appropriate radio for the set.

So, she said, "ah, you want to rent them a radio." Then she put her finger to her nose which was like the sign the con men gave each other in The Sting.

So, I said yes, because I didn't really want to explain the Goodfellas debacle to Gladys. She stood there for a second, and I was sure she was going to ask me for a cut, but I guess she was getting enough for the rental and maybe she wasn't that greedy after all. So, she did that thing with her finger and her nose again and said she would take care of it.

And take care of it she did because damn if I didn't get a knock on the door three hours later, and it was not the prop guy but a prop gal, and I'm not even sure if either is politically correct. Either way, I opened the door and she said, "I've come for the radio."

I said, "ok."

And then she said, "I can't do more than $800."

I said that was fine because I would have paid her to get one of my radios in the movie. I was going to give it to charity or maybe buy new golf clubs - I wasn't sure yet.

The prop person, yeah, that sounds better, then told me the movie takes place in 1953 and the director was all about authenticity so I gave her a very thorough tour of all the radios I had in the 1949-1953 range and she took a bunch of pictures and said she would consult with the director and get back to me.

I was pretty excited about the whole thing especially after she told me that the radio would appear in a scene with the moderately famous actress.

On the way out, the prop person asked me about a radio sitting on my coffee table. I had just received it.

"Yeah," I said, "aint she a beaut. 1963 Bulova. AM/FM. Plays like a champ."

She said, "That's the one we want."

I said, "it was made 12 years after the year your movie is set in."

And she said, "nobody is going to know. I like the color. Matches," - and she said the name of the actress - her "eyes."

"Don't you have to ask the director?"

"For a radio? No. I make those decisions."

"But what about authenticity?"

"Honey," she said, "this is Hollywood. Is cash ok?"

I really liked my new golf clubs. The radio got cut from the movie. Probably for the best.

I'm back in the basement of the cottage watching another bad movie.

My sister-in-law says, "did you hear they are filming a movie in Huntsville next winter? It is set in the 1940s."

Nice, I think to myself, I've got the perfect Emerson for that.

1956 WESTINGHOUSE H589P7

So, my nephews and nieces' kids like to come over and play with the radios. They also, depending on their ages, like to play with the cases. Jojo will spend an hour putting transistors in and out of leather cases. Usually, what I do is play a song through my transmitter, tune a transistor to the right channel, and let the kids walk around with the transistors. Their parents think it is all very cute. I think. Well, best not know what I think. What I will do is show them the volume wheel so they can turn it louder or softer. But what will invariably happen is they will turn the channel knob and tune out of the station which is playing the music. Then they will come to me and, again depending on their age, will say some version of 'not working.'

So, I'm handing them radios and they are handing them back to me to fix.

It can get quite hectic.

One day, a radio disappears. This red Westinghouse:

I'm writing this on my iPhone and again I have typed *Weatinghouse* by mistake. So, I have had to go back and fix it. I collect both Westinghouse tube radios and Westinghouse transistor radios so I have to write *Westinghouse* a lot. I get it wrong about 50% of the time. And I might be being generous. Go ahead and try it. It's not easy. Then again, I am prepared to concede I might just be an idiot.

Where was I? Oh yes, the missing Westinghouse. In the morning, it is no longer in the case.

One of the kids must have wandered around the house and put it down somewhere

I'm not naming names, but I think it is Chaim, the two-year-old. The kid seems too happy to be legit.

Right now, he's my number one suspect. I'm not worried.

It will turn up.

But it doesn't.

Everyone joins in the search. We turn the house upside down.

I really like that transistor. Not only is it beautiful, but it plays great. But I don't really care. It's just a transistor. I have hundreds.

I just can't understand where it could be.

I look in the recycling and then, oh the horror, I look in the garbage bin.

We turn up no less than three baby pacifiers. I have to stop letting family stay at my house.

But no radio.

Now, the kids are 6, 4, and 2. So interrogation is out.

But I ask some questions.

It seems that the two oldest, *Survivor* style, have formed a pact. They don't say it in so many words, but their money is on the two-year-old.

The missing radio remains a mystery.

My friend, Russ Abrams, known by collectors as Transistor Man, generously and unexpectedly, sends me one for free. So, the one in the picture, is not the one currently on the display.

I'm not done questioning Chaim yet. But I have to wait until he learns how to speak.

1957 MOTOROLA IN WISTERIA LAVENDER

Allie tells me to only write about one radio in a story. She thinks that more than one radio gets confusing.

The way she says it, I get the impression she is substituting confusing for boring.

This story has two radios. But I have to tell you about one in order to tell you about the other.

But I promise to keep it short.

The 1950 Sterling Deluxe 1000 is on page 339 of Peter Sheridon's seminal book about beautiful radios.

I bid on it once and lost it so when it came up again, I decided I would win it this time. And so, I did. The seller was in Canada and he said he would pack it carefully and send it by FedEx. He also generously had the package insured. Which sounds like a good thing but it meant I would have had to be home to sign the package.

Now, I'm home all the time. So much so that my friend Fern is concerned I have turned into a shut in. Not really sure what she loves about the traffic on A1A. But I do typically golf in the afternoon, and, sure enough, when I got back one day there was a note from FedEx on the door. I was mildly irritated at myself for not having told the seller to not insure it but there was not much I could have done. So, I signed the *No Signature Required* part of the notice and stuck it to the door. Now of course the next day there was another *Sorry We Missed You* notice with the dreaded *You can pick it up at this FedEx location*. The note I had stuck on the door was lying on the doormat. Now I'm not going to pick it up at FedEx. The whole point of FedEx is they bring it to you. So, I skipped golf the next day and stood watch until I saw the tell-tale truck, and then I ran down the street to flag it down. I didn't recognize the driver, Roberto, but I somehow convinced him to back up to my house where I gave him a bottle of Evian and a short tour of the radios. I also handed him the slip. Roberto said, "next time I will text you, give me your number."

And I thought to myself, *next time?*

But I gave him my number and then I drove out to the middle of nowhere, then stood in line for 45 minutes behind a woman who was sending 29 packages to California, to pick up my Sterling 1000 and go home.

I am almost finished writing about the Sterling. I only want to add that although it was perfectly nice, with that splash of mottled blue, it was much smaller and lighter than I had anticipated and if I hadn't known better, I would have thought it was a $29.95 toaster from Walmart.

This is only to say that when, a few days later, I received a text with a picture of a radio, I could see right away it was from Roberto (FedEx).

Now if Roberto hadn't included the picture of the radio I would have thought it was a restaurant review because he spent the first two paragraphs talking about this hole in the wall place on a side street in Little Havana which only the locals knew about which made the best Cuban sandwiches.

Finally, he got around to telling me there was this very cool looking purple radio behind the counter.

I looked at the picture.

I knew this radio.

It wasn't purple.

It was Wisteria Lavender.

The radio, a Motorola, was very, very common.

But the color, what Roberto said was purple, was very, very rare.

'Wow,' I texted back, 'thank you so much for letting me know. That is a super rare radio.'

Then I hopped into my car, and drove an hour to Miami in order to eat some succulent roast pork.

So, I was in Miami and the lady in my car's GPS had basically stopped giving directions. Every time I made a turn, she said, "no dude, not a good idea."

I pulled over to ask someone and the guy looked at me like I was an idiot. I get that look a lot. So, I tried it in my mangled Spanish. I knew that ham was *jamón* so I threw that word in a lot. The guy, he was a young guy with a beard and a Miami Dolphins hat worn backwards, pointed at a sign literally above my head - *Sándwiches Cubanos*.

I said, "gracias."

He said, "fucking tourists."

The place was definitely for locals. I'm going to go ahead and say I was the only Egyptian Jew in the whole place.

There was no menu.

They only served Cuban sandwiches.

I didn't know how to say, "can you make mine with not so much pork?" So, I took a seat at the bar and held up my finger in the universal ordering sign.

"Cerveza?"

"Si," I said.

I was such a Renaissance man.

He brought me a Cristal in a can. No glass. That was fine. I could drink from a can.

I took a sip and that was when I saw it.

Behind the counter. It was playing what sounded like Spanish music but it was hard to tell with all that static.

"Sounds like that baby could use a new capacitor," I said.

Of course, I only said that in my head. Instead, I said, "nice radio."

He then turned his head and imitated a spitting motion. At least I hope he was imitating.

"It's a piece of shit. Belongs to my mother in law. She brought it back from the old country."

"I'd be happy to take it off your hands," I said trying hard not to sound like the ugly Canadian that I was.

"The minute she dies," he said, and then this time I did see spit, "you are welcome to have it. But don't hold your breath. That old tank will outlive us all."

It was nice to see such close-knit families. I could have made him an offer.

But I didn't want to be that guy.

It was only a radio.

Gotta say Roberto was right about the sandwich though. It was delicious. I was finishing the last of my beer and thinking of ordering two Cubanos to go when an older man in a porkpie hat sidled up to me.

"You like radios?" he asked.

He managed to say it in a way that sounded lascivious.

"Sure," I replied. What was I supposed to say?

And he said, "I come back."

He must have lived upstairs because he was back five minutes later holding what appeared to be a Sony Walkman.

"Fifty bucks," he said.

By now, every eye in the sandwich shop was on me. I figured this wasn't the right time to launch into a lecture about the aesthetics of mid-century moderns. Instead, I went into my wallet and gave him a fifty.

You know how at the park they have signs which say, "don't feed the pigeons."

Well, in this case, I was the only pigeon.

Within ten minutes I was conducting a Little Havana episode of Antique Road Show. There was soon a line out the door of people holding every imaginable piece of shit electronic device ever made in the 80s and 90s.

I bought it all.

I think I bought three VCRs.

Two car radios which, if they were fish, appeared to have been freshly caught.

I bought it all.

Until my wallet was empty.

Then everyone went home.

I got up to go too.

I asked if they took credit cards.

"Only cash," the guy behind the bar said with a straight face.

Then he broke out laughing.

"Just messing with you man. It's on the house. Tell your friends."

I picked up my two bags of useless electronics and, with a last look at the Motorola, walked back to my car.

Two weeks later I went back with Lewberg and Goldfarb. The sandwiches were as good as I had promised them but the radio, the wisteria lavender Motorola, was gone.

I caught the bartender's eye.

"Your mother in law?" I asked arching my eyebrows and nodding towards the empty spot the radio once held.

"Healthy as a horse," he said.

"So what happened to the radio?" I asked.

"My loco FedEx guy offered me $200 for it," he said.

"But what about your mother in law?" I asked.

"200 dude."

"But your mother in law and the old country?" I wailed.

"I bought her an iPod. She's happy as a pig in shit. Besides, she said that purple color was as ugly as Satan himself."

Not purple. Wisteria lavender. "You want a beer?" he asked.

And I said, "yeah."

Then I said, "better make it tequila."

1958 GRUNDIG MAJESTIC

Allie wants to know where the Masters story is.

I tell her the Masters story is not about radios.

She says, "A, it most certainly is about radios, and, B, when has that ever stopped you before?"

"Nobody wants to hear the Masters story," I say.

"I think they do."

"It makes me look like an idiot," I say.

"All the more reason," she replies.

So, this is the story about playing golf at Augusta National, which is where The Masters is played every year. I'm not crazy about this story. I have absolutely no problem if you decide to skip it.

Lewberg, Goldfarb, and I were watching The Masters at my house. As he did every single year, Goldfarb said, "I would kill to play there." He knew you could only play Augusta National with a member. And we didn't know any members. To give you an example, Condoleezza Rice was a member. And, as we did every single year, Goldfarb and I turned to Lewberg, and Lewberg shrugged his shoulders, shook his head, and helped himself to some more Ketel and cran. So, this time, Goldfarb and I were barely paying attention when Lewberg said, "I think I've got a guy."

Now, if Lewberg said he had a guy, then he had a guy.

But that didn't stop me from saying, "Seriously?"

And Lewberg said, "Pappy, do I lie?"

"What's the story?" I asked. So Lewberg told us.

I call Allie.

"Listen," I say, "I've got an idea."

"Did you write the story?"

"I'm working on it."

"So, what's your idea?"

"I'm thinking that the beginning of the Masters story is way more interesting than the end."

"The beginning?"

"Yeah, you know, how Lewberg met the guy at a poker game. How he loaned him money after losing an all-in bet. That story has everything. It has intrigue. It has infidelity."

"Infidelity?"

"It could have infidelity. Big gambler. Cheats on his wife."

"Just write the story."

"But the intrigue?"

"Write the story."

So, Lewberg and Goldfarb went to Georgia three days early and made a trip of it. But I couldn't go early with them because I had a friend staying over.

"Let him fend for himself," Lewberg argued.

"I can't," I replied. "He's coming from San Francisco to see me. I'm already ditching him for a day and a half."

"3 pm tee time," said Goldfarb.

"Once in a lifetime."

"I know, I know. I'm taking the first flight out. I will have plenty of time."

My friend Gary didn't golf but he understood. He owned a TV. Besides, he was staying a week, so we would have plenty of time together. He had some meetings set up and was going to see his mother-in-law. I had offered him the use of my car.

He was great company. Loved my radios. Was easy to entertain.

He was very amused that I had gotten everything ready a few days in advance. My clubs were already in the trunk because I had decided not to golf in the days before for fear of tweaking my back.

"Aren't we excited," he said with a laugh.

"I still can't believe I'm going," I replied.

"Tell me again why you aren't taking an Uber."

"I don't trust anyone at that time. I got screwed before. I'm going to drive myself."

He was a good guest, but I was a little irritated that he had come empty-handed. Staying with me for a week and nothing. We ate every meal at the club or ordered in. I never saw his wallet.

"You can't say that!" exclaims Allie.

"What can't I say?"

"That he's cheap," she says.

"But he is cheap," I retort.

"That might be, but you'll hurt his feelings."

"Jesus. You told me to write the story."

"Yes, but you don't need to be mean. At least change the name."

"Everyone will know who it is."

"That's not the point. You should change the name."

"Ok, ok."

"And the city."

"Sheesh! Ok."

So, my friend Billy was visiting from Los Angeles.

For some reason, Billy did not seem the least bit bothered about freeloading. If anything, he seemed positively giddy about it.

"Look. I'm not going to change the name," I say, "it's stupid."

"You're stupid," says Allie.

Gary asked to borrow my car one more time. It was the evening before I would be leaving to go play Augusta National.

"I need the car in the morning," I said.

"I'll be back in a few hours."

He was now grinning from ear to ear. I remembered why he was such a lousy poker player. True to his word, he was back a few hours later. He came into the house and told me to wait in the bedroom.

I said, "Gary, if it's a hooker, you've wasted your money. I'm not taking any chances the night before I play Augusta."

"Just go wait."

He told me to come out, and I saw the surprise. I felt really shitty about calling him cheap. It was a Grundig Majestic console. I knew the radio. It was a 1958 floor radio with a stunning wood finish. It was absolutely gorgeous. It was also not cheap.

"How did you carry it into the house?" It had to have weighed a ton. He showed me the trolley. "I borrowed the trolley from Fernando."

I was absolutely flabbergasted. It might have been the nicest and most thoughtful gift anyone had ever given me. And Lewberg wanted me to ditch him. I gave Gary a hug.

"And it works too," he said with yet another toothy grin.

So, we listened to it for a while until I said, "listen, I hate to blow you off like this, but I have a very early morning flight."

"Get a hole in one," he said. Maybe he didn't own a TV after all.

"So, what do you think?"

"What do I think about what?" asked Allie.

"The story."

"That's not the story," she said.

"Yes, it is," I retorted.

"No, it's not. It is only part of it."

"Most of it."

"Not the story," she insisted.

"But it ends so beautifully. Didn't you love that hug?"

"Love the hug. Finish the story."

I didn't sleep. Of course I didn't sleep. I was too excited. Way too excited. Didn't matter. I would sleep on the plane. Two-hour flight. Two-hour Uber (I know, I know, but I couldn't waste time at the car rental place) to Augusta from Atlanta. Easy. I had left myself tons of time. There was no traffic to Fort Lauderdale Airport at that time of the morning. I made great time. Not once did I think that I should have taken an Uber. Until I opened my trunk. Where I had put my clubs. Which were no longer there. Didn't take me long to figure it out. Despite upcoming evidence to the contrary, I am not a complete idiot. Gary had taken out the clubs in order to make room for the Grundig console. And, I am being charitable here, in his eagerness to show me his gift, forgot to replace them.

"Here's the thing," I tell Allie.

"What's the thing?" she says, now a little irritated.

"Unless you play golf, you can't really understand the relationship a golfer has with his clubs."

"Am I to understand that you've reached the part of the story where instead of getting on the plane and playing with rental clubs, you decide to drive back to Boca to get your own clubs?"

"Yes."

"That is my favorite part," she says.

"The thing is, unless you play golf, you're going to think I'm an idiot."

"Ya think?"

"I love my clubs. I know my clubs. I didn't want to play Augusta with rentals."

"So, you should write that."

"People are going to think I'm an idiot."

"I'm pretty sure most people already think that."

"I had lots of time to spare."

"Bye."

So, I called Gary. Voicemail. I called him 10 times. Voicemail. Goldfarb and Lewberg were already in Georgia. Who else? Maybe Art. It was pretty damn early. I looked at the time on my phone. I could make it. It would be close. But I could make it.

Ok. So I didn't make it.

I hadn't counted on the accident on the Turnpike. Or there being no other flights to Atlanta which would have gotten me there on time. The golf bag was right next to the door where Gary had left it. Was almost impossible to miss. Almost. I walked into the house.

"Hey," said Gary, "aren't you supposed to be golfing today?"

"Got rained out," I said, "thunderstorms all day."

"What a shame," he said. "Well, I'm sure you will have other chances."

"Sure," I said.

I glanced over at the Grundig.

"Beautiful radio," I said.

"You should have seen the look on your face," he said. "It was really worth all the trouble." "Yes," I replied, "it really was."

"Let's go get some food," he said, "'I'm guessing that you're buying."

"Absolutely," I replied, "you've already done more than enough."

1958 BULOVA COMET TRANSISTOR

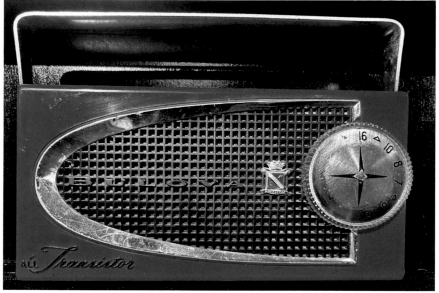

June 12, 1958

Edgar Leventine goes into Goldberg's Fine Jewelry in the Lower East Side of New York with the intention of buying his girlfriend, Esther, an engagement ring. A young lady, who is Mr. Goldberg's daughter, tells Edgar that her father went down the street to pick up an egg salad sandwich for lunch. She is just minding the store while he is gone but is not allowed to sell anything until he comes back. Mr. Goldberg is back, half eaten egg salad in one hand and a tuna salad sandwich for his daughter in the other, no more than seven minutes later. During that time, Edgar and the young lady, whose name he never learns, talk about the weather and the Yankees. She giggles twice. Esther never giggles. Edgar does not buy an engagement ring. Instead, he buys a Bulova Comet transistor, in red. He tells the young lady, who he will never speak to or see again, that he will use it to listen to baseball games.

July 4, 1958

A poker game breaks out in the basement of Esther's parents' house in Long Island after their annual 4th of July BBQ. Esther and her parents are hoping that Edgar will be taken by the festivities, and maybe the scotch, and propose. Edgar has not told Esther or her parents about his trip to the lower east side and the Bulova Comet transistor. He does not propose. Instead, he plays poker. Edgar does not really know how to play poker but he is taken a little bit by the festivities and a lot by the scotch. Also, it feels safe in the basement. His full house loses to Esther's cousin Reuben's four kings.

Reuben, and most of Esther's other cousins, are card cheats. He is disappointed that Edgar does not have enough money to cover the pot. He is also disappointed that the Bulova does not have batteries. He feels a bit bad for Edgar. What kind of fool buys a transistor radio with no batteries? He doesn't know what his cousin sees in him.

July 6, 1958
Reuben goes to a pawn shop in Jersey. It is in Mahwah and is called O'Shea's. It's a little far away but this pawn shop doesn't ask any questions. He has a few watches, some jewelry, and the red Bulova Comet transistor radio he got from cheating. He gets $20 for the Bulova.

July 7, 1958
If you are reading on in the hope of finding out what happened to Edgar and Esther, then you are shit out of luck. This story isn't about them anymore. I won't be offended if you cut your losses.

Feb 18, 1959
Katherine, little Katie, O'Shea turns 14. Her uncle, Billy O'Shea, has told her she can pick any item she wants, under $20, from the pawn shop. She chooses the red Bulova Comet.

May 20, 1959
I am born.

September 3, 1963
Katherine O'Shea gets a scholarship to attend Princeton. She is the first member of her family to attend university. The red Bulova Comet transistor does not go to Princeton with her.

Sept 7, 1963
The O'Sheas having, in a matter of four days, turned their daughter's room into a sewing room for Mrs. O'Shea, have a lawn sale consisting mostly of Katherine's old clothes, toys, and books. They get $5 for the red Bulova Comet from a man they have never seen before. He drives a hard bargain. He insists they throw in the battery for free.

Sept 7, 1963
John Kinkaid has gone to four lawn sales and five garage sales in three towns. It has been a good day. He scored a nice red Bulova Comet.

Sept 8, 1963
Edgar and Esther Levantine have their third child. A boy this time. The bris is sparsely attended because Reuben and most of the cousins are in jail.

Sept 9, 1963
Did you really think I was going to keep you hanging about Edgar and Esther?

Sept 10, 1963
Did you really think I was going to do 60 years' worth of these diaries? Let's just agree that this radio got around.

June 14, 2022
I buy the radio on eBay. The ad says radio has 'only had one owner.'

I love that.

June 28, 2022
I receive the radio in the mail. I turn it on but it makes no noise. I open it up and see the problem.

It is missing a battery.

1959 OCEANIC PIRATE 2

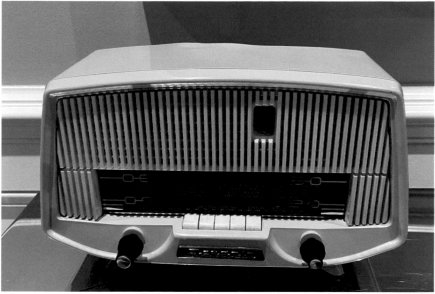

I had been dating this woman Christine, on and off, for a couple of years, and while she was generally good natured and of pleasant temperament, she had, of late, increased the amount of jokes and barbs referencing the fact that most of the Uber Eats drivers knew me by name and that I had only filled my gas tank once in three months.

Her point was well taken - I was, to be sure, a bit of a homebody and frankly, did not like to leave my radios alone for extended periods of time. I wasn't worried, like with Lewberg's dog, that left too long they might defecate on the carpet, but they could be temperamental nonetheless. So you can only imagine her joy and unbridled excitement which, to be fair only appeared after hours of hardcore scepticism, when I told her we were taking a vacation to Europe. In hindsight, I can see how the choice of the word 'vacation' might have been misconstrued. Also, and this one is on me, I probably should not have offered the hint that we were going to see one of the most famous towers in Europe.

Like I said, that one is on me.

My brother was late to his support of my radio collecting. While he too thought I was out of my mind, he decided, unlike the rest of my friends and family, not to humor me. He thought my time might be better spent running my business, in which he is a partner, rather than buying ring lights and filming thirty second clips of Frank Sinatra belting out songs from a 1952 Zenith. But seeing that he was going to be virtually alone in opposition and also realizing that his daughters were jumping in with both feet - gratefully and gracefully accepting first and then second radios, he decided to join the party. A radio, he proffered, might look good in the office.

I knew exactly what I was going to get him. He had long admired the Oceanic Surcouf that graced my living room in Florida. It was a stunning 1957 art deco piece which had been upgraded into a Bluetooth speaker. My brother, to his credit, wanted to use it as both decoration and as an everyday speaker. The sound quality was surprisingly good. I had acquired the piece from a shop in Venice which specialized in these retrofits. I spent hours on their website and finally narrowed it down to an Oceanic Pirate 2 and a very rare Pathe 450. Both French from the 1950's, and both absolutely stunning. Unable to choose, I decided to buy them both with the thought that I would take the one he liked the least.

Spoiler alert. He kept both.

Sharing my love of radios gives me immense pleasure, and so when they arrived, I asked him to take some pictures and also a few videos so I could post them on my website and YouTube. I asked for a close-up of the dial because I had, of late, developed a keen interest in the names of towns and cities displayed on these European radios. He very kindly obliged me. I then spent some time pouring over the pictures and comparing them to my very own Surcouf, and also to those of the Czechoslovakian made Tesla I owned.

I make no apologies. I like geography and I like history. I was the same when I collected stamps.

From time to time, my friend Steve will drive up and play golf with me and my friend Florida Phil. As Steve is a very slow driver and anticipates a certain amount of traffic, he generally arrives long before our appointed time. He will sometimes swim some laps, make some calls, answer emails, and then quietly and unobtrusively eat his daily lunch of a peanut butter sandwich and Greek yoghurt. This will leave him still with about 45 minutes to spare so this is when he says "any new radios?"

There is a good chance he will have left himself a note reminding himself to ask me about radios, and also a decent chance that his wife, Fern, might have called out as he left the house reminding him too. I think he was genuinely interested but I didn't really care because the number of people wanting to talk to me about radios was decreasing, so I took any opportunity I could.

Although a number of radios had arrived since he was last here I especially wanted to share the pics and radios which depicted cities and towns because Steve was also passionate about history and geography. Since he already had his nose in his phone, I texted him the close-up pics Dov, my brother, had sent me of the Oceanic and the Pathe.

"Have you even heard of all of these places?" His face was scrunched up a little, and if our friend Jeff were to walk in the room he would have said "it looks like Sof just missed a two-foot putt."

It was true. He looked like he had just missed a two-foot putt.

Because, when he said "have you even heard of all of these places," what he really meant was 'I haven't even heard of all of these places.'

Which was, as Wallace Shawn so delicately emoted in the Princess Bride, well, to him, it was inconceivable.

I opened my phone to look at the same photo he was looking at.

Here it is:

For about half a second, I harbored a sense of superiority because, as a French speaker, I suspected the French-made Oceanic would have localized French-language versions of some towns and cities, and this was perhaps what was confusing Steve. But no, even less well travelled folks than Steve would deduce that Bruxelles was Brussels. No, these were places I had never heard of.

So we looked them up.

Hilversum was a town in the Netherlands.

Beromunster was a town in a small canton in Switzerland.

And Sottens, there on the first row wedged in between Rome, Tunis and Paris, was also a town in Switzerland.

So now, I know what you are thinking. Because I would be thinking the same thing. 'Look at these narrow minded, sanctimonious, full-of-themselves, American-centric jerks .' Maybe not all of you are thinking that. But I would be.

Those towns to Europeans are very likely what Akron is to an American, or what St. Catharines is to a Canadian.

But we weren't convinced. We were, we thought smugly, too smart. So we dug a little deeper.

That is to say, we checked out Wikipedia.

Now I understand that Wikipedia is considered the low hanging fruit of the 'things you can make fun of' category. But oh, what delicious, aromatic, sweet and juicy fruit it is.

The last entry for Sottens was done in 2008. I guess there has been no need for an update in 15 years.

According to Wikipedia, the name was first mentioned in 1147 as Sotens. It has since added a T.

The population in 2008 was 257.

It was a fairly long entry for a town with only 257 people. Whoever wrote it was very precise about the population. Apparently, in that year, there had been 4 births of Swiss citizens and two deaths of Swiss citizens. So the population of Swiss citizens in Sottens increased by 2. 'At the same time, there was a non-Swiss man who emigrated to another country.' Ungrateful foreigner! It went on for five or six paragraphs outlining , in detail, other aspects of the demographics. In truth, the entry only required one line.

Because Sottens you see, in addition to having acquired an extra T to its name in the last 1000 years, also acquired what is the largest radio transmitter in all of Europe. Which is why its name appears on all these radios.

And then Steve said " You should go. It would make a good story. And I said "yeah, I should."

This is when Christine walked into the room and I turned to her and said " Hey, do you want to go to Europe and see a very famous tower?"

Now of course you all know that I did not go to Sottens. But I did ,one afternoon, to the Boca Mall to get my iPhone fixed.

Turns out people, least of all Christine, don't want to go to Sottens no matter how many t's it has.

After that, we dated more off than on.

Then only off.

I don't show Steve any more radios.

1959 CANDLE PR3

So, I'm driving on the golf course with the kids. These are my niece's kids from Chicago. We are driving up and down the fairways and they are having the time of their lives.

We get up to the green on number 12 and there is a foursome there putting, so I stop the cart by the green so we can watch. The kids have trouble believing the ball can actually go into the hole. Now these are good kids, and I have explained to them that they have to be quiet. So, we just sit there. We don't even whisper. Like I said, these are good kids.

Better than most of the members.

Anyway, one of the four gives me a stare. It's a 'what are you guys doing on my golf course' kind of stare.

So, I wave.

And he doesn't wave back. He just keeps staring. So, I wave again.

And he doesn't wave back.

So then I yell out, "what, you don't wave?" Then he waves. But he doesn't smile.

Then we drive off to number 13.

I don't think much about it, but when we get back, the kids describe the incident to their parents, and it turns out it is very possible that I might have said, "what, you don't fucking wave?"

My niece gives me her 'can you please not do that' stare, and I intimate that the kids are hopped up on soda and don't know what they are saying.

The kids don't seem that traumatized, and anyway, they are distracted because the mail has arrived and the courier has delivered three small boxes.

Transistors!

The kids are thrilled.

For some reason, they love opening the packages. Then, of course, popping the bubble wrap.

I mean, who doesn't?

They then fight over who gets to put in the 9-volt battery and then who gets to take pictures and videos of the transistor.

It's a whole thing.

They each walk around the entire house with a transistor pressed up against their ears. There's not much to listen to on AM here in Florida. Just sports or talk radio.

Doesn't seem to bother them.

I check my account on eBay to give the sellers all five-star reviews and notice that it says four transistors were delivered.

But we only got three.

I corral the kids from where they have dispersed to in the house and ask if there was another package.

They say no. Only three. Well, that happens.

Both eBay and Etsy will sometimes say a radio has been delivered, but it doesn't show up until the next day or the day after.

I check to see what radio didn't arrive. It's a working 1959 Candle. In blue. A beauty! Only $65.

My niece and her family go home to Chicago the next day and I give each kid the transistor they opened the day before.

They are thrilled.

And I wasn't so crazy about those three radios anyway. I had really been waiting for the blue Candle.

A couple of days go by and other radios arrive, and although I haven't forgotten about the Candle, I haven't done anything about it because it has only been a couple of days.

But the seller thinks it is a couple of days too long. He sends me one of these 'some of us make our living from eBay and we count on getting good reviews' diatribe. He doesn't know I give 5-star reviews for every radio I receive, regardless of the shape.

Anyway, I get it. I reply that I didn't receive it. And he says it was delivered.

I say, 'I can see it says it was delivered but I don't have it.'

Then I say, 'no worries. I'll leave a review.' I don't care.

He says, 'I have proof.'

All of a sudden, we're in an episode of LA Law.

I say, 'it's ok.'

But he wants to get to his closing argument and he sends me a picture of a package on a doorstep.

He doesn't say, 'ah hah,' but I feel it. I look at the picture.

It's not my door.

I take a picture of my door and send it to him.

I don't say, 'ah hah,' either. I just say, 'that's not my door.'

So, he then sends me a copy of the waybill with my address on it. I can see right away what he has done.

He has inverted the numbers.

So, I take a picture of my address and send it to him.

It takes about fifteen minutes but he then writes, 'I'm sorry.'

In the meantime, I have gone ahead and given him 5 stars along with a review that says, 'great radio! Great seller!' Exclamation marks are free.

I write back and say, 'no worries. It is just down the street. I'll go pick it up.'

So, I hop into my cart and drive down the street looking for the address with my inverted numbers.

I knock and of course it is the guy from the 12th green. The guy who doesn't fucking wave.

For a second, I think maybe he doesn't recognize me, but he does. So, I wave.

And he stares.

It is pretty clear we aren't going to be lifelong friends because, hey, he collects radios too. And, 'isn't that Candle a beauty?' And, 'I opened the package by mistake,' and we laugh and laugh and then drink the thirty-year-old scotch he has saved for an occasion.

None of that happens.

What happens is I say, "you got my package."

And he says, "wait here."

He comes back with a small box and says, "you have identification?" I show him my driver's license.

He doesn't say, 'Toronto, Great city. I once spent a wild weekend in Toronto.'

And then we laugh and laugh. No. He doesn't say that.

He just hands me the package and says, "one more day and I was going to toss it."

I say, "lucky for me."

I go home and put in a 9-volt battery. It plays beautifully. I take some pics and a video.

I then FaceTime my niece in Chicago. All the kids come to the phone.

I wave.

They all wave back.

That's good enough for me.

1960 ZENITH 50 TRANSISTOR

Lewberg had this childhood friend called Peter 'don't call me Pinchas' Lieberman. Neither Goldfarb nor I liked him very much. As little as we liked him, it was still more than Lewberg did. Lieberman would fly down to Miami, and Lewberg, partly out of loyalty and partly out of pity, would arrange to golf with him in the afternoon then take him out to Joe's Stone Crab down in Miami Beach for dinner. Goldfarb and I were not schlepping down to Joe's, which took no reservations, and Lewberg wasn't about to sit with him for four hours in the golf cart and then four more between the car ride and the dinner, so he called in his markers with us and we would alternate each year as to who would ride in the cart with him.

There was nothing really wrong with him but he was the kind of guy who thought conversation was just asking as many questions as possible. Most of the time, he didn't even care about the answers.

Of course, it poured once we got to number 1, and so we hightailed it back to my house to wait it out.

We were barely in the door when he started up.

"How much do you figure these radios are worth?

"Do you have insurance?"

Then fifteen minutes about his friend who had his watch collection stolen. Lewberg was hitting the Ketel and cran harder than usual and Goldfarb was the walking definition of schadenfreude.

Lieberman then got to my transistor cabinet and he did what every other five-year-old does - he opened the cabinet and started turning on radios. I wasn't sure what Lieberman's deal was, but now he was on a roll - turning on transistors, tuning into what appeared to be a Florida State sporting event - the noise was both deafening and unbelievably annoying – and then switching to the next. Then, just as quickly as he turned them on, he turned them all off and closed the case.

He looked at me and said, "22."

Then he smiled.

And I said, "22?"

And he said, "22 transistor radios playing at the same time. That's got to be some sort of world record."

By now Goldfarb and Lewberg walked into the room and joined the discussion.

"No chance that's a record," said Lewberg, "not even close."

"What do you know about it," Lieberman said, now clearly hurt.

"Just think of a Yankee playoff game," he continued, "there could easily be 1000 transistor radios listening to the game. You guys are way off."

"Seems a little random," piped in Goldfarb. "1000 individual people listening to the game; well, that's not a coordinated event. I mean, I don't think that would count."

"You see!" Lieberman poked Lewberg with the traditional 'you see' poke.

"Let's look it up," I said. And so, four more-than-middle-aged men, took out their phones and asked Google, Siri, along with Guinness and other record-keeping and world record authorities, what the record was for the most amount of transistor radios playing at the same time.

We all reached the same conclusion.

There was no record.

It did not exist.

"Doesn't that mean I now hold the record?" asked Lieberman.

And Lewberg, with a sly smile said, "no my dear Pinchas. You made a record which did not previously exist. Nobody cares about that. You know what people care about?"

We all knew the answer, even Lieberman, but it was Goldfarb who said it out loud.

"Breaking records," he said triumphantly.

"That's right Goldfarb my friend," replied Lewberg, still smiling, "breaking records."

"So," I said, working it out on the fly, "in order to be recognized we need to break an existing record?"

"That's right."

"How are we going to do that?"

And Lewberg said, "boys, the rain has stopped." But before he said that, he first said, "I think I have a guy."

Lewberg's guy, who I was pretty sure was the panhandler who worked the corner of I95 and Palmetto, had never seen a transistor before. He alternated between asking, "why is the sound so shit," and, "why don't you just use Spotify?" He also had a bit of an attitude about the lack of severity of our mission. "Lewberg," he kept saying, "this is really lame." Lewberg had said this guy was the best so I didn't beat the shit out of him. Instead, I handed him the press release I had crafted. I won't share the whole thing here but the gist of it was this:

Yvonne Goolalong Senior School in Perth, Australia celebrated their 60 years of existence by, in a touching homage to their history, playing 1963 hits on vintage transistor radios at the famed Cottesloe Beach. The hits were provided by the local radio station. And the transistors were loaned by local and very supportive radio enthusiasts and collectors. In doing so, inadvertently or not, they set the record for the greatest amount of transistor radios played at one time.

The record, one which I had made up out of thin air, was 125. I included a lovely photoshopped picture of students holding up transistors on a beach which was originally iPhones at a concert. Ain't technology grand. The picture wouldn't pass a sniff test but nobody would be sniffing.

"Aren't you being a little ambitious?" asked Lewberg.
"Gotta be a challenge," I replied, "otherwise, what's the fun in it?"

"Yeah," joined in Lieberman, "we are going to crush those wimpy Australians."

I didn't have the heart to tell him there were no Aussies.
Nor did I tell Lewberg that I didn't own 125 working transistors.

The wires printed the press release word for word. None of the legit papers or news stations picked it up, at first, but that didn't matter - if you now Googled 'world record for the greatest number of radios playing at the same time', our little fake school, complete with fake quotes from the principal and the homecoming queen, would pop up.

And, as we all knew, if it was on the internet, it was probably real. I had set the trap.

Now all I needed to do was find my fish and reel her in. But our old friend Pinchas was already ahead of me.

Neither Goldfarb, Lewberg nor I had been fraternity members. Lieberman, on the other hand, had pledged Sigma Beta Phi at the University of Michigan. He called the chapter president, who he affectionately still called his 'brother,' at the University of Miami. It took less than a week. They would team up with a sister sorority, and have a huge beach event in South Beach. All we needed to do was provide the transistors. Their chapter would handle all PR and marketing. We agreed we would share the record.

I went on an eBay buying spree.

I did not care about style, model, color or design.

I only cared if they worked.

I only cared if I could get it fast.

In the meantime, I checked my website and found the transistors I had filmed playing music. Those were the working transistors.

In the end, I had 130 working transistors.

Lewberg thought I was cutting it close.

"Lewberg," I said with a mocking laugh, "the beach is going to be teeming with bikini-clad women and strapping young men. You think there's going to be somebody there checking to see if every transistor is working?"

A Miami radio station joined in on the promotion. They refused to play hits from the 60s because it was off-brand. The record-breaking song would be from somebody called Bad Bunny.

Three TV stations showed up.

The fraternity chapter had preselected the transistor team but hundreds, maybe even a thousand, more people showed up, and a riot nearly broke out when we ran out of transistors.

Goldfarb, unusually attired in a bathing suit, said, "you know you're not going to get any of those radios back."

I had figured that.

It was, I decided, the price you had to pay for fame.

Lewberg was not in a bathing suit. I had actually never once seen him in any body of water.

But, he seemed happy enough, drinking his Ketel and cran out of a red plastic party cup.

"I can't believe you pulled this off," he said, raising his cup to salute me.

"Piece of cake," I replied, raising my own beer, "piece of history."

But Lewberg was not the only person not wearing a bathing suit. When his arm dropped after the salute, I saw a diminutive man scurrying his way towards me on the beach.

He had trouble making progress because he was wearing shoes.

Black oxford loafers.

Which matched his black suit.

He was perspiring heavily by the time he got to where I was standing. His, I have to say pasty, skin, looked like it had never encountered the sun before.

"Are you in charge of this little shindig?" he asked me in an accent I could not place.

Also, who says shindig anymore? "I am," I replied.

"Arthur Moriarty," he said, thrusting his hand for a shake. "I'm from Guinness."

"I see," I said. I had sent Guinness countless emails and letters. They had not replied to one.

"Yes," he nodded, "do you think I could have one of those beers? I'm parched."

Alanis Morissette would find it ironic that the guy from the beer company did not have a beer.

I handed him a can of beer. He took a long slug.

"Yes," he wiped his mouth as elegantly as he could, "as I was saying, I'm from Guinness. We are, of course, in charge of the integrity of the Guinness Book of World Records. Head office has sent me to monitor your event."

"Really?" I said. "That's fantastic!"

I pointed to the throngs of transistor waving people.

"As you can see. It's the real thing."

"Yes," he said. Then he sneezed. "I'm afraid the pungent scent of sunscreen is playing havoc with my allergies."

"Shame," I said, "is there something I need to sign? Do I get some sort of official document? Maybe we can take a picture?"

He sneezed again. "Yes, all in good time. But first, I need to count and test the transistors."

"You what now?"

"Have to count and test the transistors. You are claiming 130 working transistors," he had pulled out a document from a briefcase I had only just noticed, "cutting it a little close, aren't we?" Then he smiled. "The current record, of course is 125 working transistors in, let me see, Perth Australia. Lovely tennis player she was."

"Who?"

"Yvonne Goolagong. Then Cawley, of course. Are you a tennis fan? I had the good fortune to be at the Isner longest match at Wimbledon. Wasn't even my assignment. Was on vacation with the wife. I guess I was born for this job. That's what I tell the wife when she complains I travel too much. Now, maybe we can set up a little table under that umbrella. A little shade might be nice."

I have to give the fraternity brothers and sorority sisters credit. They were able to corral their transistor-holding members in fairly short time. Honestly, I don't think we lost more than two or three.

Wouldn't have mattered anyway.

Only 112 worked.

The thing is, I get no AM reception in Boca. So, a lot of the so-called working transistors were getting their signal from my home transmitter. Which had a range of about 100 feet. Now, in theory, they all should have worked because Miami has a much better signal.

But they all didn't.

To be honest, 112 was pretty impressive.

Only the Miami Herald carried the story. "Boca Raton Radio Collectors Fail in Their Attempt to Break Record." Then went on to say that an Australian high school, which I had invented, still held the record.

There's a nice picture of me holding up a 1960 Zenith Royal 50 though.

Nice radio.

Plays really nicely.

When I got home, I cracked open a beer and put on some Bad Bunny through my transmitter.

It wasn't bad. Not bad at all.

1961 ARVIN 61R13

Becky Sue Collingsworth got a transistor radio for her 14th birthday. It was a brand new in the box red Arvin. It was absolutely beautiful.

It was, by far, the worst birthday present she had ever received.

By far.

Starting in October, Becky Sue had started pestering her parents about wanting a transistor radio for her 14th birthday, which was coming up in November.

Her parents, god fearing Christians who had both been born and raised in Abilene and were both the children of ministers, had made it clear that a transistor radio, a known carrier of vile and destructive rock and roll, was not an appropriate gift for a 14-year-old girl. Most of the kids in her class had received or even bought radios long before turning 14. Even some with very strict parents. A point which Becky Sue tried to make over and over again with her parents.

"Oh Becky Sue, life was so much easier when I could just sew you a doll. I miss my little girl."

"Well, I'm not your little girl any more Mama," she replied, "I'm practically a woman."

"Oh Becky Sue," said her mother, "you will always be my little girl."

"Mama," said Becky Sue, "if you don't get me a transistor radio for my birthday, then you might as well get me nothing at all."

On the morning of the 22nd of November, Becky Sue woke up with nervous anticipation. She could smell the bacon, her favorite, and coffee in the kitchen. On the table was a small wrapped box.

It could only be one thing.

She ripped open the wrapping, dug into the box, and there it was.

A red Arvin transistor radio.

She read the model number.

61R13. It was, without doubt, the most beautiful thing she had ever seen.

She popped open the battery case and cried out, "batteries, batteries, batteries. Can I have the batteries?"

And her father said "You'll get the batteries when you turn 16."

Becky Sue's mother was looking straight down at the kitchen tiles. She could not look her daughter in the eye.

"Now Becky Sue," continued her father, "this here is a lesson. You said you wanted a transistor for your birthday. Well, you got a transistor."

"But it doesn't play without the batteries," whispered Becky Sue.

"It sure don't," he replied.

"Ok Daddy," she said, "I understand. And I love my present. Thank you very much. And thank you very much for my birthday bacon."

"You're welcome little girl."

"Two years will go by real fast, baby," said her mother, still not meeting her daughter's eyes.

Cruelty, it turned out, can come in many forms.

When she turned 15, Becky Sue ran away from home and got a ride with a trucker from Fort Worth called Brad. She packed a small bag and stuffed in the red transistor.

She travelled all over the United States, lying about her age and taking on all sorts of jobs.

She did her best to be the good lady she was raised as. But it wasn't always easy.

She brought the radio everywhere she went. Often taking it out of the box and stroking it as she would a stray cat.

But she never played it. Not once.

Twice, she bought batteries for it. Once even went as far as opening the battery case. But she never played it.

Oh, she listened to music alright. At parties and clubs. In honky-tonks and down in the common room of the YMCA in Houston.

Some rock and roll.

But mostly country music which reminded her of home in Abilene. She never played the Arvin though.

On her 16th birthday, she got up and walked to the corner store and bought herself a 9-volt cylinder battery.

She sat down right there on the curb in front of the store, unlatched the battery case, inserted the battery, and applied pressure on the tuning wheel until she heard the satisfying click of the radio turning on.

It was the news.

It sounded like something had happened in Dallas.

She turned up the volume of her transistor radio and listened.

1962 CONTINENTAL TR-682

I receive a text from Lewberg telling me that golf is at 3:00. So, I get myself a bottle of water and go to the garage to jump into the cart and drive to the first tee. That's when I see the Angel of Death. He is decked out in a Nike dry-fit shirt, Nike shorts, and a 1968 Masters golf hat which, if sold on eBay, would be described as mint. I look down at his feet, half expecting sandals, but he is wearing FootJoy golf shoes and white ankle socks. He has very graciously unplugged the long gray charging cable from the floor of the golf cart. I get into the front seat, toggle the switch from Forward to Reverse, and slowly back out of my driveway. So far, neither the Angel of Death nor I have spoken a word. I'm the first to break the ice.

"They aren't going to let you play in a collarless shirt," I say.

"Who is they?" asks the Angel of Death.

"The golf club," I reply, "they are very strict about these things."

And then the Angel of Death says, "fascists," and I laugh. If he wasn't the Angel of Death, I think we could be friends.

"I'll get you one of mine," I say.

"Much obliged," he replies.

I return with a logo shirt I got at TPC Sawgrass and gently toss it to him. The Angel of Death stares at me for a second and then makes a signal with his fingers which I understand means he wants me to turn my back. Turns out the Angel of Death is modest. I would never say it out loud, but the Angel of Death has put on a few pounds since the last time I saw him. Truth be told, so have I. He taps me on the shoulder to let me know I can turn around. The shirt looks good on him. I start driving up the 18th fairway towards the driving range. I stop in the middle of the footbridge over the pond to show the Angel of Death Iggy the Iguana.

"Never dies," he says with a shudder, "those things give me the creeps."

"What are you doing in these parts?" I ask.

"A guy can't take a vacation?" he replies with mock indignation.

"Seriously?"

"Tractor-trailer jackknifed on the Turnpike," he says.

"Jesus," I say.

"It's a living," he says without a trace of irony.

I stop in front of the free soda fountain. "You want something?"

"Lewberg will have some Ketel and cran?"

"Obviously."

"Then I'm good."

Lewberg and Goldfarb are on the driving range. I introduce the Angel of Death. Only, I introduce him as Stan. Lewberg and Goldfarb both give me a 'what in the world?' look. I'm not surprised. The boys, myself included, don't really like playing with strangers. It's a rule we don't like to break. We should probably add a rule about playing with grim reapers. On the other hand, Solly, our regular fourth, has not shown, so it turns out we need another guy to play a match.

"Where the hell is Solly?" Lewberg asks.

"Said he was feeling under the weather," answers Goldfarb.

I shoot the Angel of Death a look.

He shrugs his shoulders. "I'm off the clock, dude. People get sick."

We decide to play a cart vs. cart scramble. Nick, the starter, discreetly pulls me aside and tells me my guest has to tuck his shirt in. I tell my guest, Stan, to tuck his shirt in. He glares at Nick, but, after stalling for a second or two, reluctantly complies.

"The guy looks like he has a bad heart," he says, taking a practice swing with the driver.

"Can we just play golf?" I reply.

"Yeah, all right," he says.

I'm not sure what I expected from the Angel of Death in terms of golf, but he is perfectly fine. Neither good nor bad. If anything, he plays a lot like Solly. I text Solly just in case.

'You ok?'

'Shrimp tacos,' he replies. 'Have been on the can for two hours.'

'Serves you right for eating bottom feeders,' I text back with four laughing emojis.

'I hope you break three windows,' he texts back.

The Angel of Death curls in a 24-footer for birdie on number 2. We high-five.

"Where do you play out of Stan?" asks Goldfarb. This is likely the only small talk Goldfarb will make all day.

"Little public course in Jersey," he replies. "Pace is a bit slow, but they keep it in good shape."

"Sounds like hell," says Lewberg, pouring us all some vodka as we get to the tee on number 3.

"A little bit," says Stan. "But it's home to me."

Much like Solly, the Angel of Death hits his drive on number 4 into the water. Goldfarb gives us his ball retriever, and we fish for it in the weeds by the water's edge.

"If the boys back home could see you now," I say with a laugh as I watch him lie on his belly and stretch his six-foot frame to rescue the ball. He seems genuinely thrilled to have found the ball.

"Nice," I say.

Then he says, "I have a radio story."

And I say, "oh, here we go. I knew that something other than the pond smelled fishy."

"Accident on the Turnpike," he says. "Just thought since I was here, I could kill two birds, sorry a bit insensitive, with one stone."

"I'm good," I say. "The book is done."

"This is a great story," he replies. "Hear me out."

"The book is done," I repeat.

"Is it? Lizards in the bathtub?"

That hurts.

"You don't think it's funny?"

"I think it's hilarious. But, you know, doesn't have much edge."

"So now you want me to assail the reader with something metaphysical? Something completely out of left field? Golfing with the Angel of Death? I don't think so."

"Give your readers some credit. They are a lot more sophisticated than you think. Besides, you gotta throw them a curveball from time to time. Keeps them on their toes."

"I'm going to stick to softballs, Stan. Sorry, you're not making it into this book."

"Suit yourself," he says. "But it's about the Kennedy assassination."

"Not interested. Besides, I already have a story about the Kennedy assassination in this collection."

We play our golf and drink our vodka. The Angel of Death is perfectly affable. On number 12, he turns to me and says, "It's not actually a story."

I say, "What's not actually a story?"

"My radio story," he replies. "I said it was a great story, but it's not actually a story."

"It's not?"

"No. I mean, a writer like Calvino could make it into a great story.

Now he is just baiting me.

I, of course, take the bait.

"If it's not a story, then what is it?" I ask.

"An artifact," he says.

"An artifact?"

"A collector's item, you might say."

"A radio?"

"Transistor radio," he replies. "1962 Continental TR 682."

Lewberg screams out, "are you going to hit your damn ball or what?"

I tell him to hold his horses. Then I step up and promptly hit my ball into the water.

The Angel of Death, 5-hybrid in one hand, a transistor radio he has pulled out of his bag in the other, goes up to take his turn. He hands me the radio, then hits a beauty to within five feet.

I turn the Continental on. It has a battery in it, and I can hear some static and faint sounds of talk radio. We both get into the cart and drive to the green.

"It was in his rooming house," he says.

"Oswald?" I ask, although I already know.

"Yup."

I look at the radio, then hand it back. "I don't want this," I say. "I appreciate the gesture, but this is not for me."

The Angel of Death says, "I understand," and then, as if throwing out a runner at home, flings the transistor into the pond.

"Ok?" he asks.

"Ok," I reply.

The Angel of Death takes a sip of his drink. "Although…" he says, trailing off.

"Yeah?" I reply.

"I might have a line on an Emerson Marilyn Monroe listened to while she took a bath," he says.

"Now that," I reply, taking my own sip, "might get you into a story."

1970 AMOCO PROMOTIONAL TRANSISTOR

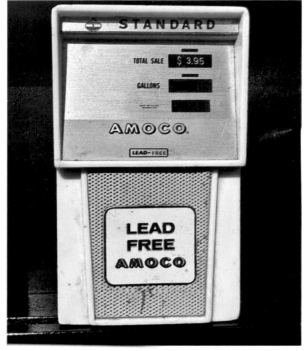

They had rehearsed it every night for a week. It was a simple plan. Pull up to the gas station in their 65 Mustang. Fill up the gas tank in order to reduce suspicion. She had come up with that one. She thought it was very clever. Who else could have thought of filling up before robbing the place? Then slowly walk in, slip on the pantyhose masks at the door, brandish the 22, take the money from the till, slowly walk back to the car, then drive away.

Easy.

Simple.

They had practiced it. They had rehearsed it. Over and over.

Not once had they talked about hitting the brakes, backing the 'Stang back up to the station, and going back to into the office.

Not once.

They had gone over a lot of different scenarios.

What if someone else is in the office?

What if there is another car?

What if the attendant refused to open the cash register?

Plus, she had made up four different escape routes.

Had rehearsed them all.

And now?

Now what?

He was going back in?

This was not part of the plan.

She knew he was too dumb to execute this plan.

She had made it as simple as possible.

But he was too dumb.

Took her two days to convince him that putting on women's pantyhose as a mask was not going to be interpreted the wrong way.

Interpreted by whom.

Jesus, he was dumb.

What was he doing in there? What was taking so long? This was not part of the plan.

He finally came out of the gas station, grinning ear to ear. He was holding a blue transistor radio.

He waved it at her.

"Free with fill-up," he said getting into the driver's seat.

"Ok," she said, shaking her head.

"We filled up," he argued, "you get a free radio with every fill-up."

"Ok," she said, "what took you so long?"

"Well," the sounds of the sirens interrupted his reply. Then flashing lights from the other direction.

"Which way?" he asked. He hadn't paid attention to the escape plans. They were all too complicated.

"Doesn't matter," she said, "just tell me why it took so long."

He pulled off to the side of the road and stopped the car.

"They gave me the yellow one," he said. "But I already had the yellow one. He had to go to the back to get the blue one." He held it up.

And she said, "ok," as the police cars surrounded them.

1975 SPIDERMAN TRANSISTOR RADIO

My friend Evie says this story practically writes itself. Maybe, but for a month now, I haven't been able to get past the first line. The story is nominally about me going on eBay in order to see if I can find a Spider-Man transistor radio for my grandnephew, Ido. Ido was here, with his sister Ella and his parents, visiting from Israel. It turned out he had a thing for Spider-Man. A little like I had a thing for radios. So I got it.

There was a tacit understanding that a visit at Uncle Ronnie's would involve a series of presents. I asked him what he wanted. He said he wanted a Spider-Man costume. Now, Ido really loves Spider-Man, and over the course of the week, I heard him say Spider-Man on dozens and dozens of occasions. He would say it very, very quickly. The opening sp would get swallowed as if a single letter, and the r was a soft r, so soft that it was nearly imperceptible. It was, as you might have guessed, crazy cute. It was also the kind of thing that I, being the cruel and cold-hearted soul that I was, might have wanted to make fun of. Thing was, Ido was a very sensitive young boy. So much so that both my sister and my nephew gave me the heads up that kids didn't get my irreverent jokes and I should try and keep them to a minimum.

I, of course, thought that was nonsensical, so the first thing I did when they walked into my house was warn them that coughing and sneezing were not permitted in the house. Two days later, Ido started crying, and when asked why he said, "I really need to cough but Uncle Ronnie doesn't let."

So, I didn't make fun of the way he said Spider-Man. Well, not for the first few days anyway.

I found a Spider-Man costume on Amazon and some sort of Barbie toy for Ella, and although I think Amazon is an evil horrible company, you have to admit their delivery is kinda superhero-like, because the packages came the next day.

Now, Ido was happy with his gift, but I could sense he was not really happy. I could understand why, because it wasn't so much a costume as a Halloween mask and a cape.

So I said, "let's see what else there is,"

Then, of course, his parents said, "no, no he loves his gift."

So I said, "well, let's see what else there is."

The kid was turning his head back and forth hoping I would be the one who won the fight.

Which, of course, I did.

Once he got the green light he proceeded to explain, again uttering the word Spider-Man many, many times, that what he wanted was a Spider-Man body suit which even went over his face.

So that's what I bought.

And since Ido was getting another present, I also got Ella a Barbie costume.

Both costumes were from eBay, so I could see that delivery, unlike Amazon, was not going to be overnight.

What you need to understand is that as a slightly out of control radio collector, I get a lot of packages delivered to the front door. Especially if I happen to be on a transistor-buying binge.

So, it got to be this daily thing where I would tell the kids to check the front door and they would drag in a box or two and hover around me as I cracked it open, and then, upon discovering it was an Arvin transistor, they would both dejectedly exclaim, "it's just one of Uncle Ronnie's radios."

Now, to be fair, both kids loved the radios. Ella and Ido even helped me to make videos. Whenever someone from Israel would FaceTime, the call would include a twenty-minute tour of the radios.

"Wait, wait Bubby," Ella would say, "there are more in this room." I'm just saying they really loved the radios.

But they were kids waiting for presents, and so, "it's just one of Uncle Ronnie's radios," became a recurring line at the house.

I then thought, how funny would it be if one of Uncle Ronnie's radios was a Spider-Man transistor radio? Could such a thing exist?

I mean seriously, how good would that be! Admit it, that's pretty good right?

So I went on eBay.

Took ten seconds of searching before I found it. A Spider-Man transistor radio. Perfect. And yeah, yeah, yeah, I got a Barbie transistor radio too.

The costumes arrived a few days later. Ido wore his to bed. He wore it to the Boca Town Center.

The transistors, unfortunately, arrived the day after they left. So, I didn't get my aha moment.

This is what happens when you write the truth instead of making things up.

'This story just writes itself,' said Evie.

If you want, you can take a moment and try to picture Ido's face when he says, "it's just one of Uncle Ronnie's radios," and then realizes it is a Spider-Man transistor radio.

Look at that face. He can't really believe what is going on. He stares at his parents with a look of disbelief. Is this really happening? Then we rip open the box, I go get some batteries, and the transistor radio, the Spider-Man transistor radio, comes to life.

Would have been great. But, none of that happened.

I shipped the transistors to Israel. The shipping cost was more than the price of the transistors.

I sent the story to my family.

The general consensus was that my story sucked. My family had suffered three collections of almost the truth.

"It could have been so good, Uncle Ronnie," said Danna.

"I don't get it," said Rena, "you just had to stretch the truth a little bit."

"Seriously Uncle Ron?" said Rachel. Sammy was not as diplomatic.

"What the hell dude," she said, "now you decide to tell the truth? What the hell! You ruined what could have been a great story."

Only Ido was happy.

His parents read him the story.

He couldn't believe there was a story about him. He didn't need to be tricked by a contrived tale. For him, the truth was pretty great.

"Read the part about me coughing again," he said. "Uncle Ronnie is always joking. That is my favorite part."

1940 EMERSON PATRIOT REDUX

Every once in a while, I try to summit Everest without the use of supplemental oxygen. And every time I try, my trusty Sherpa has to drag my ass back to base camp 4. Now, as you all know, I am about as likely to climb Everest as I am to climb a flight of stairs if an elevator is nearby - but it is sometimes how I feel when I try to write a story without adding a little bit of a lie.

To me, the lie is just that extra oxygen I need to get to the top.

The lie is the pair of scissors you use to snip off a part of the last piece of the puzzle so it fits just right.

This collection features stories about radios. In some, they play a major role. In others, they are a minor, although important, part. Once in a while, I may have tried to force an ill-fitting part of the puzzle.

The story I am about to tell has nothing to do with radios.

Not even a little bit.

So, it was not going to make it into the collection.

Then, last Thursday, the Eddie Murphy movie, *Coming to America*, was on TV. And it reminded me of this story.

This story which had no radios and no lies.

Now, I have no problem lying, but all around me I have seen other writers scale Everest without the aid of supplemental oxygen, so I wanted to try too.

Of course, I could tell the story without including a radio and even start a brand-new collection, but that really sounded like a lot of work, so first I decided to see if I could somehow fit a radio into the story.

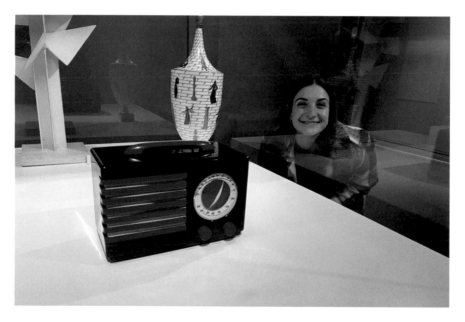

This is a picture of my niece Danna at the Metropolitan Museum in New York. She is posing behind a 1940 Emerson Patriot designed by Norman Bel Geddes. When I first started collecting radios, I asked Danna how many would be reasonable. She answered that any more than ten would be whack. If you haven't figured it out by now, let me be clear, I have more than ten.

Now, although mine is a different color, I have the exact same radio she is posing next to and the fact that it is in the Met maybe makes me seem a little less whack. I sent this picture to my friend Tatiana, who is designing the coffee table edition of this book, and she said, 'wow, it is a little eerie that you send me this picture on the same day I am designing the Emerson Patriot story.'

And I said, 'yes. Eerie.'

I'm not sharing this anecdote because I wanted to insert a radio into the story.

No.

I'm sharing it because I wanted to insert the eeriness. Pay attention. Keep alert. It doesn't get easier.

Now the story I want to tell is about a French painter named Maurice Utrillo. In my first collection, I have a story about how my parents had an Utrillo reproduction in their house and how, every time I was in Paris, I would try to see as many Utrillos as I could and how, one time, with my friend Carainn, we went to an actual Utrillo exhibit and I ended up finding the exact painting we had in our house. If this all sounds all a little sentimental, that is because it is.

Part of the conceit of this story, and what you need to know, is that, although Utrillo is a painter of some renown in the art community, he is not very famous in the manner of a Renoir or Degas or Matisse, whose works and styles are instantly recognizable. Utrillo was known for his paintings of street scenes of Montmartre, in Paris.

The other thing you need to know is that when I came back from Paris, I somehow got it into my head that I was going to buy an original Utrillo. It did not take long for me to come back to earth and realize I could not afford an original Utrillo. What I could afford, and only barely at that, was the work of a 20th century painter, also French, by the name of Antoine Blanchard. Blanchard, whose name came up in Google as, 'if you like Utrillo but have no money you might also like,' painted turn of the century Parisian street scenes. As he was born in 1908 and died in 1988, the scenes he painted were not live but were in fact inspired by postcards of the time.

I had never bought art before which did not feature dogs playing poker, so it took me quite a while to pull the trigger, but I did end up buying a beautiful nighttime snow scene.

Here it is:

Ok, so I think you now have enough of the background.

I'm going to start telling the story. As I start to type, let me be honest and say it still does not have a radio in it.

I'm in my house in Boca and I'm working on the edits of the story Looking for Maurice, which is my story about Maurice Utrillo.

I get a text from my friend Allie and she tells me she is about to watch *Coming to America*. She makes it sound like someone is forcing her to watch it.

Now I have watched *Coming to America* many times. It is with Eddie Murphy and Arsenio Hall. I think it is very funny.

So I turn it on.

I tell Allie I am going to watch it.

Allie says that I already missed the topless scene.

I say I'm going to watch it anyway.

Like I said, I've seen it many times and I'm working on the story edit. So, I'm really only paying partial attention to the screen.

You know how you do when you are multi-tasking.

Which is why it is weird that I even noticed this.

If you've never seen *Coming to America*, then the only thing you need to know is that John Amos plays the father of the woman Eddie Murphy has a crush on. The Amos character owns a fast food restaurant called McDowell's, which is an unabashed rip off of McDonald's. There is a scene in his house when the camera focuses on a painting on the wall. The movie shows it in full for a second and I had to go back and forth with the remote in order to pause it at the exact right time.

Here is the picture I took of my TV screen.

John Landis was the director of the movie. Here's the joke he is making. Amos is a little bit nouveau riche. He has commissioned an artist to paint a Montmartre street scene and has added, in a manner we are supposed to think is crass and unsophisticated, the storefront design of his own restaurant - McDowell's.

The painting is on the screen for no more than a second. Maybe two.

I look at it and, if not for the fast food sign, think it could be an Utrillo.

I don't want to throw shade on Landis but it might have been funnier if he used a very recognizable impressionist painting.

But that's just me.

Still, although you have to be paying attention, it is a funny bit.

Now go to the picture and zoom in on the signature on the bottom right corner.

Do you see it?

McTrillo.

Landis, or maybe the set designer, or maybe the prop person, has created a painting for the movie and has taken the joke so far that he has changed Utrillo to McTrillo.

A very minor French painter nobody who ever went to go see *Coming to America* in the theaters had ever heard of.

You can't see the signature unless you pause the movie.

McTrillo.

On the day I am editing my Maurice Utrillo story.

The way I see it, and tell it, in 1988 John Landis included an inside joke in a movie that I, and only I, would understand in 2020.

Which is, in a word, eerie. So that's the story.

No word of a lie.

For what it's worth.

But it still doesn't include a radio.

Which is a bit of a shame, because I think it is a pretty good story.

Now, I could lie. It would be easy to throw in a store selling vintage radios in Montmartre. Maybe owned by Utrillo's great grandson. That could work. But I promised myself I would make the summit without the extra oxygen.

Where was I going to find a radio which was going to be a fit for this story?

So, I go to eBay.

I don't even know what I'm looking for.

It's ridiculous.

I start searching through the listings of tube radios. I try tube radios manufactured in France.

But nothing that fits.

It is hopeless.

Maybe just a little oxygen I think to myself. Just a breath or two.

It is hopeless.

I'm ready to give up.

Even if I find something, I don't even know what, how is it going to help the story. I can see we are almost at the end.

On a whim, in desperation, I type in Novelty Transistor Radios. A duck radio.

A windmill radio.

A, hand to god, Kraft Macaroni and Cheese radio.

And then I see it.

It is a painting which also works as a transistor radio. Manufactured by the Futura Corporation of St Louis Missouri.

Here, take a look.

Damn if it isn't our old friend Antoine Blanchard.

So, I buy the radio.

And I buy the batteries.

It plays great.

I put on Charles Aznavour singing La Boheme. It is a song about the good old days in Montmartre.

Then I go write my story.

FAVORITES FROM THE COLLECTION

1938 Crosley Model G1465 'Split Grille', yellow tortoise

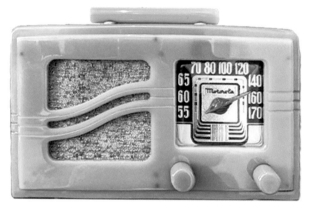

1939 Motorola Model S grille Catalin, green

1940 Addison Model A2 Catalin, navy swirl

1940 Emerson Model 400 'Aristocrat', bright green

1940 Crosley Model 646C 'Super Sextette', red

1940 AMC Model 126 Ring Catalin

1941 Sonora Model KM Catalin, amber brown

1941 Emerson Model 5 Plus 1 Catalin

1941 Philco Model 42KR

1945 Sentinel Model 284 'Wavy Grille'

1946 FADA 'Bullet' Model 1000 Catalin

1946. Air King Model A600 'Duchess'

1947 Detrola Model 568 Chrome AMSW

1947 Westinghouse Model 4H-126

1947 Coronado Model 43-8190

1948 Philco 'Flying Wedge'

1949 Coronado 'Moderne'

1950 Lang Model 122

1948 Madison Model 940

1950 Coronado 'Moderne'

1950 Northern Electric 'Midge Bullet'

1950 Tesla Talisman Model 306U

1950s Arvin Model 451T, blue

1950s Sparton football

1951 Zenith 'Consoltone' Model H511

1951 Crosley 'Bulls Eye'

1951 Zenith Model L723 AM/FM

1952 Admiral Model 6C23N-P

1952 Hallicrafter Model 5R20

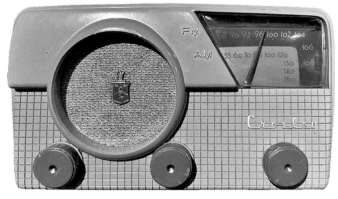

1953 Crosley Model E30TN AM/FM

1954 Crosley Model E10BE

1953 Emerson Model 744B

1953 Motorola Model 53HW

1953 Philco Model 53-563

1953 Zenith Model K412-Y Owl Midget

1954 Olympic Model 441, Maroon

1954 Packard Bell

1954 Hallicrafters Model 612

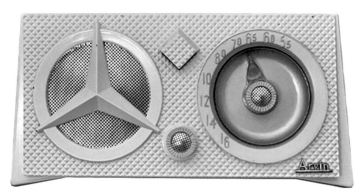

1955 Arvin Model 855T Tri-Star Ivory and Gold

1955 Motorola Model 56H 'Torpedo' Green

1955 RCA Victor Model 6X8B The Wilshire

1955 Stewart Warner Model 9187

1955 Zenith Model R519F Kelly Green

1955 Zenith Model 511V Broadway

1956 Hallicrafters

1957 Motorola Model 57H Azure Blue

1957 Motorola Model 57H Sea Green

1957 Olympic Model 408

1957 Silvertone Harmony House Model 8027

1957 Motorola Model 57R4 pastel pink

1959 Arvin 'Tri-Star' Mercedes

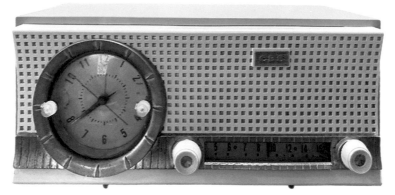

1959 CBS Model C230 Grasshopper Green

1959 Mercedes Plakson

1959 Musicaire Model MD-300 'Bumble Bee'

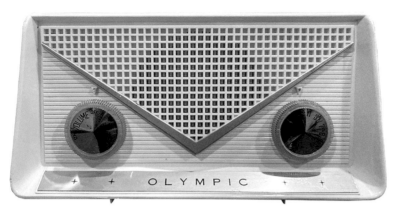

1959 Olympic Model 550 'Cadillac'

1959 Olympic Model 552

1959 Zenith Model R519V Hot Pink

1960 General Electric Model T165A

1963 Bulova Model 370 AMFM

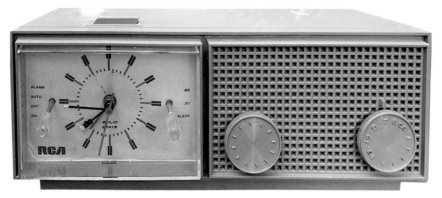

1966 RCA Model RLO21A Cobalt Blue

ABOUT THE AUTHOR

Aaron Zevy is the author of Almost the Truth: Stories and Lies, *The Bubbe Meise and Other Stories, Not Book Club Material*, and *Schlepping Across the Nile: Collected Stories. Radio Daze: A Descent Into Collecting*, is his fifth book.